Elizabethan England

Design by John Rushton Associates
Picture research by Procaudio Ltd
Maps by Tim Smith

Holmes McDougall Ltd, Allander House,
137-141 Leith Walk, Edinburgh EH6 8NS

SBN 7157 1563-1

Acknowledgements

The Project team would like to thank the following
trial school teachers for their help in preparing
sections of this book:

N. T. Malden, Bishop Vesey's Grammar School,
Sutton Coldfield, Birmingham
Miss C. Folkard, Thorpe Grammar School, Norwich
Mr N. A. Moxon, Bradford Grammar School,
Bradford, West Yorkshire
Mrs P. Hesketh, Arthur Mellows Village College,
Peterborough.

Project team

David Sylvester (Director to 1975)
Tony Boddington (Director from 1975)
Gwenifer Griffiths (1975-1976)
William Harrison (1972-1975)
John Mann (1974-1975)
Aileen Plummer (from 1972)
Denis Shemilt (Evaluator from 1974)
Peter Wenham (1972–1974)

Printed in Great Britain by
Holmes McDougall Ltd, Edinburgh.

Schools Council
History 13-16 Project

Enquiry in depth

Elizabethan England

RIGHT: Bull and bear baiting, a
contemporary woodcut

Contents

The Tudors 1485-1603

Henry VII = Elizabeth of York *d. 1503*
1485-1509 *daughter of Edward IV*

Arthur
d. 1502

Henry VIII
1509-1547

James IV = (1) Margaret (2) = Archibald Douglas
of Scotland *Earl of Angus*

Mary (1) = Louis XII
of France

(2) = Charles Brandon
Duke of Suffolk

Mary = James V
of Guise *of Scotland*

Margaret = Matthew Stuart
Earl of Lennox

Philip II = Mary
of Spain *1553-1558*
(by Catherine
of Aragon)

Henry Fitzroy
illegitimate

Elizabeth
1558-1603
(by Anne
Boleyn)

Edward VI
1547-1553
(by Jane
Seymour)

Henry Grey = Frances
Duke of
Suffolk

Eleanor = Henry Clifford
Earl of Cumberland

Margaret
d. 1596

Francis II = (1) Mary Queen (2) = Henry Stuart
of France of Scots *Lord Darnley*
d. 1560 *Ex. 1587* *d. 1567*

Lady Jane Grey
Ex. 1554

Catherine
d. 1568

Mary
d. 1578

(3) = James Hepburn
Earl of Bothwell
d. 1578

James VI *of Scotland, I of England*
1567-1625

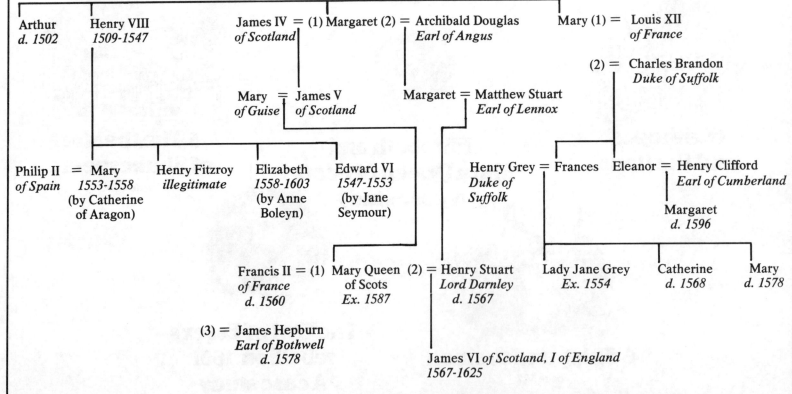

1
England in 1558

Elizabeth was proclaimed Queen of England when her sister, Mary Tudor, died on Thursday 17 November, 1558.

Her reign was a period of great contrasts. Many people grew wealthy, but beggars were a common sight. The standard of drama reached splendid heights but the audience which enjoyed Shakespeare's plays also crowded into the arena to watch dogs baiting bears and other animals. Many men, both Catholic and Puritan, were willing to face persecution for their religion, yet there was a widespread slackness in attitude about worship and church-going. English sailors showed dash and enterprise in their voyages of exploration, but Elizabeth herself was extremely cautious in her foreign policy.

Above all, it was a period of achievement. England overcame the difficulties that faced her in 1558 both at home and abroad. She was to emerge through the years of Elizabeth's reign as strong, prosperous and independent. Towards the end of the reign, one of Elizabeth's subjects wrote:

ABOVE: The rich man and the poor man, a contemporary woodcut

As your Majesty hath been a mirror to all the world for excellent gifts of mind, person, and fortune; so your reign most happy both for victorious arms, and flourishing arts, which shall remain glorious to all posterity . . .

The Queen

The glamour which we associate with Elizabethan England was always apparent in Queen Elizabeth I. Through the Court she created it was to spread to the rest of the nobility in England, but there was little evidence of it in 1558. It is difficult to

imagine exactly what Elizabeth Tudor looked like. Although there are many portraits of her, she sat for very few of them. The majority are copies of others so we do not know how lifelike they are. Written accounts of her appearance vary, but she was consistently described as a striking young woman with a commanding presence (sources 1-4). We know that she took great pride in her clothes and loved ornaments and jewels. These displayed her wealth and status as well as symbolising her importance.

SOURCE 1 The Venetian Ambassador describes her as a young woman

. . . she is now about twenty-one years old; her figure and face are very handsome, and such an air of dignified majesty pervades all her actions that no-one can fail to suppose she is a queen.

Rawdon Brown (ed.), *Calendar of State Papers, Venetian*, Vol. V, London, 1864-1898, p. 539

SOURCE 2 A different Venetian Ambassador describes her two years later

. . . she is now twenty-three years old . . . although her face is comely rather than handsome, she is tall and well formed, with a good skin, although swarthy; she has fine eyes and above all a beautiful hand of which she makes a display.

Brown, *State Papers, Venetian*, Vol. VI, p. 1058

SOURCE 3 A Scottish envoy from Mary, Queen of Scots describes Elizabeth in 1564

The Queen [Elizabeth] said she had clothes of every sort; which every day thereafter, so long as I was there, has changed. One day she had the English Weed, another the French, and another the Italian, and so forth. She asked me which of them became her best. I answered, in my judgement, the Italian dress; which answer I found pleased her well; for she delighted to show her golden coloured hair, wearing a caul and bonnet as they do in Italy. Her hair was more reddish than yellow, curled in appearance naturally. She desired to know of me, what colour of hair was reputed best; and whether my Queen's [Mary's] or her's was best; and which of the two was fairest. I answered, the fairness of them both was not their worst faults. But she was earnest with me to declare which of them I judged fairest. I said, she was the fairest Queen in England and mine the

ABOVE: Elizabeth I, the Rainbow portrait, c. 1600, attributed to Isaac Oliver

LEFT: Elizabeth I, the Ermine portrait, 1585, attributed to Nicholas Hilliard

PAGE 8 TOP: Henry VIII
PAGE 8 BOTTOM: Anne Boleyn

fairest Queen in Scotland. Yet she appeared earnest. I answered they were both the fairest ladies in their countries; that her Majesty was whiter, but my queen was very lovely. She enquired which of them was of highest stature. I said, my Queen. Then, saith she, she is too high; for I am myself neither too high nor too low.

Sir James Melville, *Memoirs of His Own Life*, Chapman & Dodd, 1922, p. 55

SOURCE 4 A German visitor to England in 1598 describes her in her old age

. . . next came the Queen, in the sixty-fifth year of her age, as we were told, very majestic; her face oblong, fair, but wrinkled; her eyes small, yet black and pleasant; her nose a little hooked; her lips narrow, and her teeth black (a defect the English seem subject to, from their too great use of sugar); she had in her ears two pearls, with very rich drops; she wore false hair, and that red; upon her head she had a small crown, reported to be made of some of the gold of the celebrated Lunebourg table; her bosom was uncovered, as all the English ladies have it till they marry; and she had on a necklace of exceeding fine jewels; her hands were small, her fingers long, and her stature neither tall nor low; her air was stately, her manner of speaking mild and obliging. That day she was dressed in white silk, bordered with pearls of the size of beans, and over it a mantle of black silk, shot with silver threads; her train was very long, the end of it borne by a marchioness; instead of a chain, she had an oblong collar of gold and jewels.

Paul Hentzner, *Travels in England in the Reign of Queen Elizabeth*, Cassell, 1889, pp. 47–8

BELOW: The Queen proceeding to Westminster

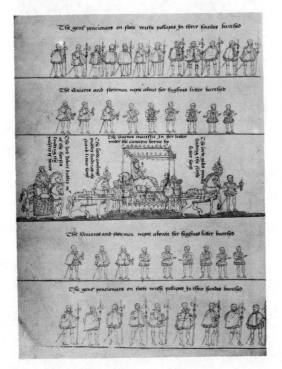

The coronation

From the first month of her reign she showed herself frequently to her subjects. Before her coronation she was to be seen riding through the streets of London and in her state barge on the River Thames. She made a solemn progress through the City of London to Whitehall for her coronation. It was an elaborate affair, costing at least £16 000 (source 5). Events included pageants before and at the time of the coronation and a great banquet in Westminster Hall for the Court and nobility which lasted from 3.00 p.m. to 1.00 a.m. The coronation ceremony at Westminster Abbey was seen by as many people as possible. It was a solemn and magnificent occasion.

Timber was brought up from the Windsor forest for seating. Other materials were shipped over from Antwerp, the great luxury emporium of north-west Europe. The Yeomen of the Guard got new scarlet coats, with silver and gold spangles. All the household, down to the jesters, Will and Jane Somers, were measured for new clothes; the thirty-nine ladies who attended Elizabeth were each provided with sixteen yards of velvet, plus two yards of cloth of gold; the senior officers of the state had crimson velvet and the Privy Councillors crimson satin. Elizabeth herself had four state dresses made: one, for her procession through the City, of twenty-three yards of gold and silver, with ermine trimmings, and silver-and-gold lace coverings. Her coronation robes, with their great cloak of ermine and embroidered silk, can still be seen in her official portrait, but she had two other state dresses, of crimson and violet velvet, and changed her outfit twice during the ceremony.

Paul Johnson, *Elizabeth: A Study in Power and Intellect*, Weidenfeld and Nicolson, 1974, pp. 67-8

BELOW: Roger Ascham

Her education

Elizabeth's glamour is not only explained by her looks and social graces, she was also highly intelligent and very well educated. She had been taught by some of the greatest scholars of the time, including Roger Ascham, who was a very gifted teacher. Elizabeth learned to read Greek and Latin, and spoke French and Italian fluently (source 6). She also mastered the religious debates which occupied so many of the scholars of her day. She was an accomplished musician and seems to have been quite athletic; riding and hunting appeared regularly on the Court's list of activities.

SOURCE 6 **Princess Elizabeth at the age of twenty-three**

Her intellect and understanding are wonderful, as she showed very plainly by her conduct when in danger and under suspicion. As a linguist she excels the Queen [Mary Tudor], for besides Latin she has no slight knowledge of Greek, and speaks Italian more than the Queen does, taking so much pleasure in it that from vanity she will never speak any other language with Italians.

Brown, *State Papers, Venetian*, Vol. VI, pp. 1058-9

Early experiences

Elizabeth had also learned much before she came to the throne about the dangers of being at the centre of power. When she was a child of two her mother, Anne Boleyn, had been beheaded. Elizabeth herself had been imprisoned during Mary's reign and she learned that her life depended on confiding in no one and trusting very few people. She saw how some people were tempted to use the heir to the throne in their plots against the sovereign. She had been suspected of being involved in plots against Mary Tudor and she was determined that during her reign there should be no obvious person around whom plotters could gather. Although she was only twenty-five when she became Queen, she was in many ways discreet and wise.

ABOVE: Mary Tudor

Elizabeth's accession

From the early 1570s the anniversary of Elizabeth's accession was celebrated as a public holiday and from 1576 it was added to the list of holy days. But on the accession day itself in 1558 the mood was rather different. The death of Mary Tudor might have been greeted with relief by many people, but amongst the powerful and important there was anxiety, even pessimism (sources 7, 8).

If Elizabeth put a foot wrong she could find herself at war with Scotland, France or Spain. There were already people willing to challenge her claim to the throne, and they could provide alternative candidates, the most powerful of whom was Mary, Queen of Scots. Even if Elizabeth could keep her throne, there was the fear that she might follow her sister Mary's example and marry a foreign prince, bringing England under the influence of a foreign country.

SOURCE 7 A description of England in 1558 by one of Elizabeth's Privy Councillors who had also served Edward VI

The Queen poor, the realm exhausted, the nobility poor and decayed. Want of good captains and soldiers. The people out of order. Justice not executed. All things dear . . . . Wars with France and Scotland. The French king bestriding the realm, having one foot in Calais and the other in Scotland. Steadfast enmity but no steadfast friendship abroad.

Armagil Waad, 'Distresses of the commonwealth', in Henry Gee, *The Elizabethan Prayer Book*, London, 1902, p. 211

SOURCE 8 In 1560, Sir Thomas Smith, a Protestant and one of the Queen's most trusted Councillors, recalled the situation in England at Elizabeth's accession

I never saw . . . England weaker in strength, men, money, and riches . . . As much affectionate as you [know] me to be to my country and countrymen, I assure you I was then ashamed of both . . . They went to the wars hanging down their looks. They came from thence as men dismayed and forlorn. They went about matters as men amazed, that wist not where to begin or end. And what marvel was it? . . . Here was nothing but fining, heading, hanging, quartering and burning; taxing, levying and pulling down of bulwarks at home, and beggaring and losing our strongholds abroad. A few priests, men in white rochets, ruled all; who with setting up of six-foot roods and rebuilding of rood-lofts, thought to make all cocksure.

John Strype, *The Life of Sir Thomas Smith*, Oxford, 1820, pp. 248-50

2
The structure of government

England in 1558 was a weak country compared with her European neighbours, France and Spain. It was clear that to survive the early years of the new reign, strong government was essential. Elizabeth was a glamorous, intelligent and dedicated queen but she needed the support of the people, Parliament and her ministers to form a strong government. Although the institutions of government in Elizabethan England were similar to those existing today, the balance of power between them was different. As Queen, Elizabeth herself was the source of power.

The government

Ministers were chosen in a very different way and had different powers and responsibilities from those of today. There were no political parties as such and the Queen herself chose ministers and officials to advise her (sources 9, 10). They were all part of the Court, the great retinue of men and women who surrounded the Queen at Whitehall or her other palaces.

SOURCE 9 **Elizabeth's address to the House of Lords at her accession**

I shall require you all, my lords, (chiefly you of the nobility, everyone in his own degree and power) to be assistant to me; that I with my ruling, and you with your service, may make a good account to Almighty God . . . I mean to direct all mine actions by good advice and council.

Sir John Harington, *Nugae Antiquae*, Vol. I, London, 1804, p. 67

PAGE 14: Elizabeth I being carried by her courtiers, c. 1600, attributed to Robert Peake

SOURCE 10 Elizabeth chose her Councillors herself

. . . for counsel and advice, I shall accept you of my nobility, and such others of you the rest, as in consultations I shall think meet, and shortly appoint; to the which, also, with their advice, I will join to their aid and for ease of their burden, others meet for my service; and they which I shall not appoint, let them not think the same for any disability in them, but for that I consider a multitude doth make rather disorder and confusion than good counsel . . .

Harington, *Nugae Antiquae*, Vol. I, p. 67

RIGHT: Elizabeth I with some of her advisers

The Court

People came to Court hoping to be noticed by the Queen (source 11) and to be given some appointment which would bring them an income and greater status. This way of making appointments is called patronage. People saw the Queen as their patron. They were likely to be loyal to her in the hope of being given further positions or for fear of being dismissed. Not everyone at Court approached the Queen for appointments; many would hope to be given jobs, or recommended for appointments by one of the already famous and powerful men who were close to her. Many regarded other leading courtiers such as William Cecil or the Earl of Leicester, as their patrons. But the Court, with its network of patronage, was not enough to keep the whole country loyal and obedient to the Queen.

Although the Court was the centre of affairs of state (source 12), there was a more formal organization to see that the country was properly governed. A government must make the laws, ensure that they are enforced and punish those who break the laws.

The Privy Council and Parliament were concerned, amongst other things, with the making of laws. How they were carried out depended very much on local officials in the counties. The most important of these were the Justices of the Peace. Finally, to deal with law-breakers, there were different courts of law.

SOURCE 11 Lord Herbert of Cherbury recalled his arrival at Court in 1600

As it was the manner of those times for all men to kneel down before the great Queen Elizabeth, . . . I was likewise upon my knees in the presence-chamber, when she passed by to the Chapel at Whitehall. As soon as she saw me, she stopped, and swearing her usual oath demanded, "Who is this?" Everybody there present looked upon me, but no man knew me, until Sir James Croft, a pensioner, finding the Queen stayed, returned back and told who I was, and that I had married Sir William Herbert of St Julian's daughter.

Sidney L. Lee (ed.), *The Autobiography of Edward, Lord Herbert of Cherbury*, London, 1886, pp. 81-2

SOURCE 12 Elizabeth's Court

The court over which [Elizabeth] presided resembled a large family, with its members closely knit by ties of kin and the obligations of allegiance. As a family it had its feuds, where personalities clashed, its favourite sons with their nicknames, and its ill-favoured daughters. Factions—the ancestors of political parties—developed round leading courtiers, and Elizabeth sought to maintain a nice balance to keep the peace. As a matriarch she expected these her "relations" to be about her, justifying aristocratic privilege by personal service.

This was, on the face of it, a compact society comprising privy councillors, peers, and senior officials both of the royal Household proper and of the departments of state that had technically broken away from it, and the wives of some of the great men held posts as ladies of the Bed Chamber or Privy Chamber, or found a niche for a daughter or a niece as a maid of honour. Though servants of the crown were entitled to board and lodging at court, their wives could not expect to share this privilege as of right and whatever exceptions the Queen made, the rule itself remained.

Neville Williams, *All the Queen's Men*, Cardinal, 1974, p. 14

The Privy Council

This was a small body of the Queen's most important ministers. It met regularly and often followed the Queen in her travels around the country. In her sister Mary's reign the Privy Council had had as many as fifty members, but Elizabeth chose to keep her Council small. Numbers varied from twelve up to about twenty, but it was usual for only five or six to attend meetings. Its principal task was to advise the Queen on important questions of state, so it was essential that its members should be able to work together. At the same time it was important that they should represent different shades of opinion so that Elizabeth might have as wide a view as possible of what people with influence and power thought about different issues. Then it would not appear that she was listening to only one group of people (sources 13,14). Elizabeth kept fewer than a third of Mary's old Privy Councillors, and many of those she kept because she felt they could be useful to her.

Elizabeth moved cautiously, appointing Councillors who were all experienced in affairs of state. However, the youngest of them at her accession was the most influential. There was no sixteenth-century equivalent of the modern prime minister, but the position which provided the widest view of all government business was that of the first Secretary of State. On the day she became Queen, Elizabeth appointed William Cecil to this position. He was then thirty-eight (source 15).

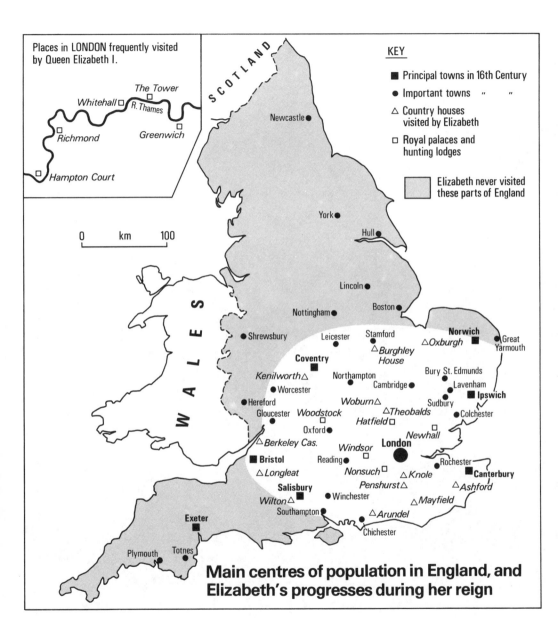

Places in LONDON frequently visited by Queen Elizabeth I.

The Tower
Whitehall
R. Thames
Richmond
Greenwich
Hampton Court

SCOTLAND

KEY

■ Principal towns in 16th Century
● Important towns "   "
△ Country houses visited by Elizabeth
□ Royal palaces and hunting lodges

Elizabeth never visited these parts of England

0   km   100

Newcastle

WALES

York
Hull

Lincoln
Boston
Nottingham

Shrewsbury
Leicester
Stamford
Norwich
△Oxburgh
Great Yarmouth

Coventry
△Burghley House
Northampton
Bury St. Edmunds
Kenilworth△
Cambridge
Lavenham
Worcester
Woburn△
Ipswich
Hereford
Sudbury
Gloucester
Woodstock
△Theobalds
Colchester
Hatfield
Oxford
Newhall
△Berkeley Cas.
Windsor
London
Longleat
Reading
Nonsuch
△Knole
Rochester
Canterbury
Bristol
Penshurst△
Ashford
Salisbury
Wilton△
Winchester
△Mayfield
Exeter
Southampton
△Arundel
Chichester
Plymouth
Totnes

Main centres of population in England, and Elizabeth's progresses during her reign

ABOVE: Sir William Cecil, Lord Burghley

19

SOURCE 13 The Privy Council was sometimes divided in its advice to the Queen.

. . . Leicester, Hatton and Walsingham have endeavoured to persuade the Queen that it is desirable for her to openly take the states [the Netherlands] under her protection . . . but they have been opposed by Cecil and Sussex when the matter was discussed in the Council, and the question therefore remained undecided.

M. A. S. Hume (ed.), *Calendar of State Papers, Spanish*, Vol. III, Elizabeth, p. 346

SOURCE 14 The work of the Privy Council

This day [15 April 1582] the Lords and others of her Majesty's Privy Council considering what multitude of matters concerning private causes and actions between party and party were daily brought unto the Council Board, wherewith their Lordships were greatly troubled, and her Majesty's special services oftentimes interrupted . . . it was agreed among them that from henceforth no private causes arising between parties for any action whatsoever . . . shall be received and preferred to the Board, unless they shall concern the preservation of her Majesty's peace or shall be of some public consequence . . .

John Roche Dasent (ed.), *Acts of the Privy Council*, New Series, Vol. XIII, HMSO, 1896, pp. 394-5

SOURCE 15 Elizabeth appoints Sir William Cecil as a Councillor

I give you this charge, that you shall be of my Privy Council, and content yourself to take pains for me and my realm. This judgment I have of you, that you will not be corrupted with any manner of gift, and that you will be faithful to the state, and that, without respect of my private will, you will give me that counsel that you think best, and if you shall know anything necessary to be declared to me of secrecy, you shall shew it to myself only, and assure yourself I will not fail to keep taciturnity therein. And therefore herewith I charge you.

Harington, *Nugae Antiquae*, Vol. I, pp. 68-9

William Cecil and his rivals

In many ways William Cecil (who was created Lord Burghley in 1571) was an obvious choice. At Cambridge he had been educated with some of Elizabeth's future tutors and by the age of twenty-seven he had attracted enough attention to be brought into Henry VIII's service. He

PAGE 20: Elizabeth I, surrounded by her Privy Councillors, receives foreign ambassadors

seemed to have certain important things in common with Elizabeth. He too had been imprisoned in the Tower of London, and, like the Queen, he seemed to value outward conformity in religious beliefs. They shared a strong desire to make their country prosperous, united and respected. Cecil was able to provide the practical knowledge on how to go about this, as he had more experience than Elizabeth about how the government worked. They also agreed that there should be a balance of opinions and attitudes within the Privy Council.

The Earl of Leicester

This principle of balance seemed to be threatened when Elizabeth had been seriously ill with smallpox in the autumn of 1562. She pressed her Councillors that if there should be any such emergency in the future, Lord Robert Dudley, later Earl of Leicester, should be appointed Protector of the Kingdom. Most people at Court believed that Elizabeth was in love with Dudley as she spent much of her time with him. In October 1562 he was made a Councillor. Cecil was understandably anxious about his own position, but also about restoring the balance, which seemed about to be upset by Dudley's increasing influence.

It was with this in mind that Cecil persuaded the Queen to appoint the Duke of Norfolk to the Privy Council at the same time as Dudley. There is no doubt that, during much of the 1560s the Queen

ABOVE: Lord Robert Dudley, Earl of Leicester, c. 1565
ABOVE RIGHT: Thomas Howard, 4th Duke of Norfolk

turned constantly to Dudley for advice. She made him Earl of Leicester in 1564 and by 1569 many people who disliked Cecil's policies regarded Leicester as their leader. But, perhaps because of his relationship with the Queen, his popularity did not last and long before his death in 1588, he had ceased to be a real threat to Cecil's power. Cecil retained a unique position of power and influence until his death in 1589.

The Earl of Essex

Another of Elizabeth's favourites, the Earl of Essex, seemed to present a challenge in Cecil's last years but Elizabeth was not

LEFT: Robert Devereux, 2nd Earl of Essex

prepared to grant her favourite the political power he wanted, see 'The Earl of Essex's rebellion, 1601 : A case study'. While Cecil had been an incomparable servant to Elizabeth she was not prepared to raise one man up to a position of power over the whole of the Privy Council (sources 16-26).

SOURCE 16 A description of Sir William Cecil by a fellow Councillor

. . . in the Queen's entrance [when Elizabeth became Queen] he was admitted Secretary of State; afterwards he was made Master of the Court of Wards, then Lord Treasurer, for he was a person of most excellent abilities; . . . and so I conclude to rank this great instrument amongst the Togati, [the senators] for he had not to do with the sword, more than as the great paymaster and contriver of the war which shortly followed, wherein he accomplished much, through his theoretical knowledge at home and his intelligence abroad, by unlocking of the counsels of the Queen's enemies.

Sir Robert Naunton, *Fragmenta Regalia*, London, 1641, p. 131

SOURCE 17 A conflicting contemporary description of Sir William Cecil

The principal person in the Council at present is William Cecil, now Lord Burghley, a knight of the garter. He is a man of mean sort, but very astute, false, lying and full of all artifice. He is a great heretic and such a clownish Englishman as to believe that all the Christian princes joined together are not able to injure the sovereign of his country, and he therefore treats their ministers with great arrogance.

Hume, *State Papers*, *Spanish*, Vol. II, p. 364

SOURCE 18 A contemporary description of the Earl of Leicester

He was a very goodly person, tall, and singularly well featured, and all his youth well-favoured, of a sweet aspect, but high-foreheaded, which (as I should take it) was of no discommendation; but towards his latter, and which with old men was but a middle age, he grew high-coloured . . .

Naunton, *Fragmenta Regalia*, p. 125

BELOW: Lord Robert Dudley, Earl of Leicester, c. 1576

SOURCE 19 Another description of the Earl of Leicester, written in 1559

. . . a very handsome young man . . . towards whom in various ways the Queen evinces such affection and inclination that many persons believe that if his wife, who has been ailing for some time, were perchance to die, the Queen might easily take him for her husband . . .

Brown, *State Papers, Venetian*, Vol. VII, p. 81

SOURCE 20 A foreign view of the Privy Council, an account written to Philip II, King of Spain in 1571 by the Spanish Ambassador, De Spes

This man [Cecil] manages the bulk of the business, and, by means of his vigilance and craftiness, together with his utter unscrupulousness of word and deed, thinks to outwit the ministers of other princes. This to a certain extent he has hitherto succeeded in doing. Next after him, the man who has most to do with affairs is Robert Dudley, Earl of Leicester, not that he is fit for such work, but because of the great favour with which the Queen regards him. He is a light and greedy man who maintains the robbers and lives by their plunder. He is ungrateful for the favours Your Majesty has granted to him and is greatly inclined to the French party, from whom he receives an allowance. The other man who has his hand in the government is the Lord Keeper, or guardian, as they call it, of the Great Seal [Sir Nicholas Bacon]. He is an obstinate and most malignant heretic, and, being Cecil's brother-in-law, always agrees with him. The Admiral [The Earl of Lincoln] does not interfere very much in arranging matters, but he is a very shameless thief, without any religion at all, which latter may also be said of the Earl of Sussex.

The latter also belongs to the Council and is a more capable man than any of the rest. He has shown signs sometimes of wishing to serve your Majesty, as he is an enemy of the Earl of Leicester. The Earl of Bedford also belongs to the Council. In person and manners he is a monstrosity and a great heretic. There are others of less authority than these men, lawyers, creatures of Cecil, who only repeat what he says. They have recently admitted James Croft into the Council; he is secretly attached to the Catholic party and your Majesty's service, but dares not speak very openly . . .

Hume, *State Papers, Spanish*, Vol. II, p. 364

BELOW: The Spanish Ambassador to England in 1564

ABOVE: Sir Francis Walsingham

SOURCE 21 A description of Sir Francis Walsingham

Doubtless he was the only linguist of his times, how to use his own tongue, whereby he came to be employed in the chiefest affairs of State . . .

At his return [from being Ambassador to France] he was taken principal Secretary, and for one of the great engines of State, and of the times, high in his mistress's [the Queen's] favour, and a watchful servant over the safety of his mistress.

They note him to have certain courtesies and secret ways of intelligence above the rest; but I must confess that I am to seek wherefore he suffered Parry (the traitor) to play so long as he did, hang on the hook, before he hoisted him up.

Naunton, *Fragmenta Regalia*, pp. 139-40

SOURCE 22 She did not allow any of her ministers to become too powerful

Her ministers and instruments of State . . . were many, and those memorable; but they were only favourites, and not minions; such as acted more by her princely rules and judgments, than by their own wills and appetites . . .

The principal note of her reign will be, that she ruled much by faction and parties, which she herself both made, upheld, and weakened, as her own great judgment advised . . .

Naunton, *Fragmenta Regalia*, pp. 103-4

SOURCE 23 She treated her advisers rudely at times

When the Queen heard this she turned to Secretary Walsingham, who was present, and said a few words to him which the shipmaster did not understand; after which she threw a slipper at Walsingham and hit him in the face, which is not a very extraordinary thing for her to do, as she is constantly behaving in such a rude manner as this.

Hume, *State Papers, Spanish*, Vol. III, p. 573

SOURCE 24 Another example of her rudeness to a minister

Her temper was so bad that no Councillor dared to mention business to her, and when even he [Cecil] did so she had told him that she had been strong enough to lift him out of the dirt, and she was able to cast him down again.

Hume, *State Papers, Spanish*, Vol. IV, p. 87

SOURCE 25 Elizabeth took the credit for any successes that were achieved

Her wisest men and best councillors were oft sore troubled to know her will in matters of state; so covertly did she pass her judgment, as seemed to leave all to their discreet management; and, when the business did turn to better advantage, she did most cunningly commit the good issue to her own honour and understanding; but, when aught fell out contrary to her will and interest, the council were in great strait to defend their own acting and not blemish the Queen's good judgment.

Harington, *Nugae Antiquae*, Vol I, p. 357

LEFT: Elizabeth I gives audience to two Dutch ambassadors in the Privy Chamber

SOURCE 26 Walsingham explains to Leicester why he has not received more advice from the Council (1586)

I have let my lords here understand, how unkindly your lordship taketh it that you hear so seldom from them, and that, since your charge here you never received any letter of advice from them. They answer, as it is truth, that, her majesty retaining the whole direction of the causes of that country to herself and such advice, as she receiveth underhand, they know not what to write or to advice. She can by no means . . . endure that the causes of that country [the Netherlands] should be subject to any debate in council, otherwise than as she herself shall direct, and therefore men forbear to do that which otherwise they would.

John Bruce (ed.), *Correspondence of Robert Dudley, Earl of Leicester, during his government of the Low Countries, 1585–86*, Camden Society, First Series, Vol. 27, 1844, p. 237

BELOW: Westminster, detail from an engraving by Hollar, c. 1647

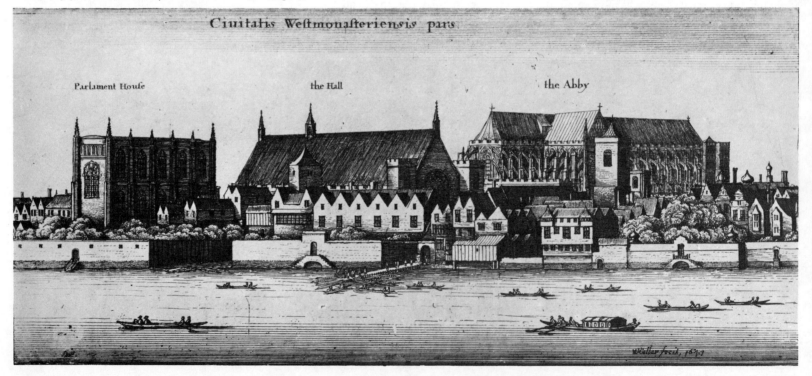

Ciuitatis Weſtmonaſteriensis pars

Parlament Houſe   the Hall   the Abby

Parliament

This was a much larger body than the Privy Council. It consisted of the House of Lords, with about 90 members, and the House of Commons, with rather more than 400 members. Elizabeth always made sure that some of her Privy Councillors were elected to the House of Commons. Their presence in the Commons was one of the ways in which she was able to influence what happened in Parliament.

Unlike the Privy Council, Parliament did not meet regularly. Some of Elizabeth's parliaments lasted for only a few months and there were long gaps when no Parliament met. This meant that it could not deal with the day-to-day business of the country. Much of the time was spent in exchanging information. Privy Councillors explained their policies and listened to what members could tell them about opinion in different parts of the country.

Its functions

Parliament had two major functions: to raise any extra money which the Queen might need over and above her normal income, for instance if she wanted to send troops abroad, and to pass laws.

Although the Queen had the power to issue proclamations, it was more usual for these to explain and justify royal action than to direct people to do things. If the Queen wanted to be absolutely certain that something had the force of law, she had to get it passed by both Houses of Parliament. A Bill became law only after it had been read and debated three times in both Houses and was then agreed to by the Queen. Although Elizabeth needed the consent of Parliament for her wishes to become unquestionable law, it could not make laws without her approval, and she did not always give her consent to the bills presented to her (sources 27-32).

SOURCE 27 The dates of Elizabeth's Parliaments

The several days on which every Parliament or session of Parliament during the reign of Queen Elizabeth began, as also the several days of the dissolution and prorogation of the same.

25th January 1559 – 8th May 1559	18th February 1576 – 15th March 1576	4th February 1589 – 29th March 1590
12th January 1563 – 10th April 1563	16th January 1581 – 19th April 1583	19th November 1592 – 10 April 1593
13th September 1566 – 2nd January 1567	23rd November 1584 – 14th September 1586	24th October 1597 – 9th February 1598
2nd April 1571 – 29th May 1571	29th October 1586 – 23rd March 1587	27th October 1601 – 19th December 1601
8th May 1572 – 13th June 1572		

Sir Simonds D'Ewes, *A Compleat Journal of the Votes, Speeches, Debates, both of the House of Lords and House of Commons throughout the whole reign of Queen Elizabeth of Glorious Memory*, London, 1693, Preface

SOURCE 28 Elizabeth's principal reason for calling Parliament in 1559

Now the matters and causes whereupon you are to consult, are chiefly and principally three points. Of those the first is of well making of a uniform order of religion, to the honour and glory of God, the establishing of the Church, and Tranquility of the Realm.

D'Ewes, *Journal of the Parliaments of Elizabeth*, p. 11

SOURCE 29 Elizabeth's usual reason for calling Parliament was the need for extra taxation; for example, in 1589, after heavy expenses were incurred in defeating the Spanish Armada

This Parliament was summoned about three months after God's miraculous preservation of Religion, the Realm and Her Majesty's person, from the ambitious and bloody conquest of the Spanish King; and therefore the House [took care for] the public safety of Her Majesty and Realms by aiding her Highness with the unusual and extraordinary gift of four fifteenths and two tenths and two entire subsidies . . .

D'Ewes, *Journal of the Parliaments of Elizabeth*, p. 428

SOURCE 30 The authority of Parliament

The most high and absolute power of the realm of England consisteth in the Parliament . . .

And, to be short, all that ever the people of Rome might do . . . the same might be done by the parliament of England, which representeth and hath the power of the whole realm both the head and the body. For every Englishman is intended to be there present, either in person or by procuration and attornies . . . from the prince to the lowest person of England. And the consent of the parliament is taken to be every man's consent.

Sir Thomas Smith, *De Republica Anglorum, A Discourse on the Commonwealth of England*, L. Alston (ed.), Cambridge University Press, 1907, pp. 48-9

SOURCE 31 Members of the House of Lords, whether members of the Church or secular nobility, are each summoned to Parliament by separate letter

The Prince [the Queen] sendeth forth his prescripts or writs to every duke, marquess, baron, and every other Lord Temporal or Spiritual who hath voice in the parliament, to be at his great council of Parliament such a day (the space from the date of the writ is commonly there at least forty days):

Smith, *De Republica Anglorum*, pp. 49-50

ABOVE: The Queen in Parliament

SOURCE 32 The members of the House of Commons are elected

[the Queen] sendeth writs to the Sheriffs of every shire to admonish the whole shire to choose two knights of the parliament in the name of the shire . . . likewise to every city and town which hath been wont to find burgesses of the parliament, so to make election that they might be present there at the first day of parliament. The knights of the shire be chosen by all the gentlemen and yeomen of the shire . . . likewise by the plurality of the voices of the citizens and burgesses to the burgesses elected.

Smith, *De Republica Anglorum*, p. 50

Elizabeth and her Parliaments

Traditionally there were certain subjects which Parliament was not supposed to discuss unless invited to do so by the sovereign. The most important of these were religion, the succession and foreign policy. However, during Elizabeth's reign the Commons made repeated attempts at discussing these subjects, especially the question of the succession. Early in the reign they had pressed Elizabeth to marry (source 33). Even when it became clear that she would not marry and have children, they urged her to name her successor. Quite apart from their genuine concern about such matters, the Commons became increasingly interested in their own privileges and began to demand freedom of speech, or the right to discuss whatever issues they thought were important.

Elizabeth continued to resist these pressures, using her charm as well as sheer stubbornness. But disputes with her Parliaments, particularly towards the end of her reign, were one of the greatest causes of irritation and distress to her (sources 34-36).

SOURCE 33 Her answer to Members of Parliament when they urged her to marry

For I assure you . . . I will never in that matter [the question of her marriage] conclude anything that shall be prejudicial to the Realm. For the well, good and safety whereof, I will never shun to spend my life and whomsoever my chance shall be to light upon, I trust he shall be such, as shall be careful for the Realm, as you . . . And albeit it might please Almighty God to continue me still in this mind, to live out of the State of Marriage, yet it is not to be feared but he will so work in my Heart, and in your Wisdom, as good Provision by his help may be made, whereby the Realm shall not remain destitute of an Heir . . .

D'Ewes, *Journal of the Parliaments of Elizabeth*, p. 46

SOURCE 34 One of the Privy Councillors ensures that the Commons choose the Speaker whom the Queen wants

. . . the Knights, Citizens, and Burgesses departing to their own house, did there take their several places, and most remaining silent, or speaking very submissively, Mr Treasurer of the Queen's House, standing up uncovered did first put the house in remembrance of . . . her Majesty's pleasure that they should choose a Speaker . . . he thought it his duty to take that occasion to commend to their choice, Sir Thomas Gargrave . . . he said he did not intend to debar any other there present, from uttering their free opinions, and nominating any other whom they thought to be more fitting . . . [They] did with one consent and voice, allow and approve of Mr Treasurer's nomination and elected the said Sir Thomas Gargrave . . .

D'Ewes, *Journal of the Parliaments of Elizabeth*, p. 40

SOURCE 35 Elizabeth's reply to demands for freedom of speech

. . . For freedom of speech her Majesty commandeth me to tell you that to say yea or no to bills, God forbid that any man should be restrained or afraid to answer according to his best liking, with some short declaration of his reason therein, and therein to have a free voice, which is the very true liberty of the House; not, as some suppose, to speak there of all causes as him listeth, and to frame a form a religion or a state of government as to their idle brains shall seem meetest. She sayeth no king fit for his state will suffer such absurdities . . .

J. E. Neale, 'The Lord Keeper's speech to the parliament of 1592-3'. *English Historical Review*, xxxi, 1916, pp. 136-7

SOURCE 36 A Bill becomes law

. . . All bills be thrice in thrice diverse days read and disputed upon, before they come to the question . . .

The last day of that Parliament or session the Prince cometh in person in his Parliament robes, and sitteth in his state; all the upper house sitteth about the Prince in their states and order in their robes. The speaker with all the common house cometh to the bar . . . Then one reads the title of every act which hath passed at that session, but only

ABOVE: Proclamation by the Earl of Sussex declaring that the Earls of Northumberland and Westmorland were traitors, 1569

in this fashion: "An act concerning such a thing etc." It is marked there what the Queen doth allow, and to such she saith "La Roigne le Veult" [the Queen wants it] . . . To those which the Queen liketh not she saith, "La Roigne s'advisera" [the Queen will consider it].

Smith, *De Republica Anglorum*, pp. 57-8

Justices of the Peace

The Queen had a personal representative in every county. He was called the Lord Lieutenant. Very often he was in London for most of the year and his Deputy supervised those who were really responsible for law and order throughout England and Wales.

These were the Justices of the Peace. Four times a year they sat in courts of law called Quarter Sessions to deal with criminal business, but they were constantly dealing with less serious offences. In addition to seeing that proclamations and laws were carried out, they were responsible for a wide range of things, from the repair of bridges to the licensing of ale-houses.

Although the Government depended on J.P.s, they were not paid. There was no shortage of men willing to do the work, because it did have its rewards. J.P.s were chosen from amongst the local gentry and it was a sign that a man was regarded as one of the leading figures in his area if he became one. The social status which the position gave them meant more than any financial payment would have done (sources 37-42).

SOURCE 37 The kind of men appointed to be Justices of the Peace

The Justices of the peace be men elected out of the nobility, higher and lower, that is the Dukes, Marquises, Barons, Knights, Esquires, and Gentleman, and of such as be learned in the laws.

Smith, *De Republica Anglorum*, p. 85

SOURCE 38 The powers of the J.P.s

. . . to the end that our justices of the peace may be able to deliver justice they are accomplished with double power . . . that is to say, with ample authority not only to convert the persons but also (after the cause heard and adjudged) to constrain them to the obedience of their order and decree.

William Lambarde, *Eirenarcha*, 1581, London, 1599, p. 60

PAGE 35: Title page of Sir Simonds D'Ewes *Journal*

QUEEN ELIZABETH IN PARLIAMENT

A L. Chancellor B. Marquesses, Earles & C. Barons D. Bishops, E. Iudges, F. Masters of Chancery G. Clerks H. Speaker of y Com
I. Black Rod K. Serieant at Armes L. Members of the Commons house M. S. Francis Walsingham Secretary of State.

A Compleat

JOURNAL

OF THE

Votes, Speeches and Debates,

BOTH OF THE

HOUSE of LORDS

AND

HOUSE of COMMONS

Throughout the whole Reign of

Queen ELIZABETH,

Of Glorious Memory.

Collected by that Eminent Member of Parliament;

Sir SIMONDS D'EWES, Baronet.

Published

By *PAUL BOWES*, of the Middle-Temple Esq;

LONDON,

Printed for *Jonathan Robinson* in St. *Pauls* Church-yard, *Jacob Tonson* in *Chancery-lane*, *A.* & *J. Churchil* in *Pater-noster-Row*, and *John Wyat* in St. *Pauls* Church-yard, MDCXCIII.

SOURCE 39 Examples of the tasks placed upon the J.P.s by various laws

No person which shall retain any servant shall put away his said servant, and no person retained according to this statute shall depart from his master, mistress or dame before the end of his term, upon the pain hereafter mentioned, unless it be for some reasonable cause to be allowed before two justices of the peace . . . the said justices . . . and other officers shall appoint convenient places to settle the same poor people for their habitations and abidings . . . and shall also number all the said poor people and thereupon set down what portion the weekly charge towards the relief and sustentation of the said poor people will amount unto . . . and they shall tax and assess all the inhabitants . . . to such weekly charge as they and every of them shall weekly contribute towards the relief of the said poor people . . .

Statutes of the Realm, Vol. IV, London, 1819, pp. 415, 593

Proclamation concerning Corn and Grain 1544

. . . [many] persons . . . have by divers and sundry means accumulated and gotten unto their hands and possession a great number and multitude of corns and grain, far above the necessary finding of their household . . . without bringing any part or parcel thereof into any market to be sold, intending thereby for to cause the prices of corns to arise . . . all justices of peace . . . shall with all convenient speed search the houses, barns and yards of such persons as have been accustomed or used to sell corns or grain . . .

Paul L. Hughes & James F. Larkin (eds.) *Tudor Royal Proclamations*, Vol. I, Yale University Press, 1964, pp. 343-4

SOURCE 40 The J.P.s in action

Robert Ringwood brought in a certain indenture wherein Lewis Lowth . . . was bound to him to serve as a prentice for seven years. And Mr John Holdiche came before the Mayor and other Justices and declared that the said Lewis is a bondman to my Lord of Norfolk's grace, and further that he was brought up in husbandry until he was 20 years old, whereupon he was discharged of his service.

W. Hudson & J. C. Tingey (eds.), *Records of the City of Norwich*, Vol. II, Norwich, 1910, p. 180

SOURCE 41 Extracts from the journal kept by William Lambarde, a J.P.

1581. August. Sir Thomas Cotton, Sir Christopher Alleyn, Thomas Willughby, Robert Richers, and I sat at Borough Green for the allowance and disallowance of alehouses, where we took bond of Roger Meare of Mereworth, tippler, for keeping good order in his ale-house, he being bound in £10 and John Betts and William Ramkyn of Mereworth aforesaid, his sureties, each in £5.

23 August. Sir Christopher Alleyn, my father-in-law, and I joined in the examination of eight persons that counterfeited their apparel and language as the rogues called Egyptians were wont to do, and we sent them to the gaol.

1583. 23 February. Sir Christopher Alleyn and I examined sundry persons at Sevenoaks concerning the suspicion of willful poisoning of William Brightrede by Thomas Heyward and Parnel, his now wife, then wife of the said William.

20 July. At Cobham Hall my Lord, Sir Christopher Alleyn, and I wrote to all the constables of this division to notify the taxation of the money for the gaol and the house of correction.

William Lambarde, 'An Ephemeris' in Conyers Read (ed.), *William Lambarde and Local Government*, Cornell University Press, 1962, pp. 21, 27, 29

SOURCE 42 The Privy Council rebukes the J.P.s of Norfolk for their slackness

. . . Whereas you received letters from us eight months since to make careful and present enquiry and certificate of all the full members and quantities of provisions taken for Her Majesty's house and stable . . . And for that we understand not of any performance by you of this her Majesty's commandment and pleasure, . . . we will and require you in her Majesty's name that presently you do proceed to the diligent execution and performance of our former letters.

H. W. Saunders (ed.), *The Official Papers of Sir Nathaniel Bacon of Stiffkey, Norfolk, as Justice of the Peace 1580-1620*, Camden Society, Third Series, Vol 26, 1915, p. 64

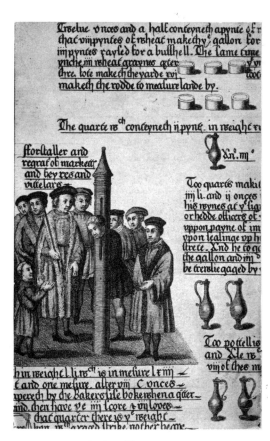

ABOVE: A man in the pillory

Courts of Law

Common and prerogative law courts

There were two kinds of courts of law. The three main common law courts were: the King's Bench, Common Pleas and the Court of Exchequer. In these courts an absolutely correct statement had to be made about the crime of which the defendant was accused. If any of the details could be shown to be wrong, the case would be dropped. If it proceeded, the accused would be tried by a jury (sources 43, 44).

The other kind of court was a prerogative court, such as the Court of Star Chamber. Here the procedure was quite different from that in a common law court. Its purpose was to make sure that powerful subjects did not overawe a jury. A written bill had to be presented, saying what the crime was, or what the quarrel was about. Each side then had to answer questions under oath (sources 45,46).

SOURCE 43 There were three courts of common law

In that hall [Westminster Hall] be ordinarily seen 3 Tribunals or Judges' seats. At the entry on the right hand, the common place, where civil matters are to be pleaded, specially such as touch lands or contracts. At the upper end of the hall, on the right hand, the king's bench, where pleas of the crown have their place. And on the left hand sitteth the Chancellor accompanied with the master of the Rolls . . . and certain men learned in the civil law called Masters of the Chancery . . .

Smith, *De Republica Anglorum,* p. 68

SOURCE 44 In common law courts, cases were heard before a jury

The sheriff always warneth 24 men to appear, lest peradventure any might be sick or have a just cause of absence . . .

When it is thought that it is enough pleaded before them, and the witnesses have said what they can, one of the Judges with a brief and pithy recapitulation reciteth to the 12 in sum the arguments of the sergeants of either side, that which the witnesses have declared, and the chief points of the evidence shewed in writing, and once again putteth them in mind of the issue . . . Then there is a bailiff charged with them to keep them in a chamber not far off without bread, drink, light, or fire until they be agreed upon one verdict.

Smith, *De Republica Anglorum,* p. 69

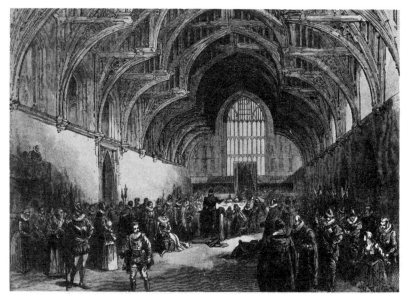

ABOVE LEFT: The Court of Star Chamber
ABOVE: A trial in progress, Westminster Hall

SOURCE 45 A prerogative court, the Court of Star Chamber

. . . every week once at the least, (which is commonly on Fridays . . .) the Lord Chancellor, and the Lords and other of the Privy Council, so many as will, and other Lords and Barons, which be not of the Privy Council, and be in the town, and the Judges of England, especially the two chief judges, from 9 of the clock till it be 11 do sit in a place called the star chamber, either because it is full of windows, or because at the first all the roof thereof was decked with images of stars gilted.

Smith, *De Republica Anglorum*, pp. 115-16

SOURCE 46 The accused was not tried by a jury in the Court of Star Chamber

There is plaints heard of riots . . . And further because such things are not commonly done by mean men, but such as be of power and force and be not to be dealt withal of every man, nor of mean Gentlemen; if the riot be found and certified to the King's Council . . . the party is sent for, and he must appear in this star chamber, where seeing as it were the majesty of the whole Realm before him, being never so stout, he will be abashed . . . he shall be so charged with such gravity, with such reason and remonstrance, and of those chief personages of England, one after another handling him on that sort, that what courage so ever he hath, his heart will fall to the ground.

Smith, *De Republica Anglorum*, pp. 116-17

Fines and punishments

It was usual for large fines to be imposed, though these were often paid in instalments, rather than in one enormous lump sum. As the number of cases brought before the law courts increased greatly in the sixteenth century, the Queen made a lot of money from the profits of these law courts. The lawyers made money too, from the fees they charged for each case.

It is not surprising that the courts took on as much business as they could handle, and sometimes more. In theory different courts were supposed to handle different kinds of cases, but in practice each court dealt with whatever business it could. In addition to heavy fines, sentences were often severe. Corporal punishments of various kinds were commonly used (sources 47-49).

BELOW: Corporal punishments
BELOW RIGHT: Punishment of prisoners in Lollard's Tower

SOURCE 47 Rogues and beggars were discouraged by stern punishment from roaming the countryside

. . . if he happen to be convicted for a vagabond . . . he is then immediately adjudged to be grievously whipped and burned through the gristle of the right ear with a hot iron of the compass of an inch about . . . If he be taken the second time, he shall be whipped again, bored likewise through the other ear, and set to service; from whence if he depart before a year be expired and happen afterwards to be attached again, he is condemned to suffer pains of death as a felon . . .

William Harrison, *The Description of England*, 1586, George Edelen (ed.), Cornell University Press, 1968, pp. 185-6

SOURCE 48 Punishments were severe for ordinary crimes

For any felony, manslaughter, robbery, murder, rape, and such capital crimes as touch not treason . . . we have by the law of England no other punishment, but to hang till they be dead . . . heading, tormenting, demembering, either arm or leg, breaking upon the wheel, impaling, and such cruel torments as be used in other nations by the order of their law, we have not . . .

If the wife kill her husband she shall be burned alive. If the servant kill his master, he shall be drawn to the place of execution on a hurdle. Poisoners, if the person die thereof, by a new law made in King Henry the Eighth's time shall be boiled to death.

Smith, *De Republica Anglorum*, p. 104

SOURCE 49 Punishment for treason was especially severe

The same order touching trial by inquest of 12 men is taken in treason, but the pain is more cruel. First to be hanged, taken down alive, his bowels taken out and burned before his face, then to be beheaded, and quartered and those set up in diverse places.

Smith, *De Republica Anglorum*, pp. 106-7

Beggers Bush.   A Maundering Begger.   A gallant Begger.

Beggers all.

42

❧ 3 ❧
The poor

One problem which concerned the Privy Council Parliament and the J.P.s throughout Elizabeth's reign was the growing number of poor people in the country. There must have been many very poor people who we know nothing about as their families or friends looked after them, so they never came to the notice of the officials. The poor who seemed to the Government to be a problem were the beggars, or vagrants—those who wandered from place to place.

Why were there so many beggars at this time?

Beggars did not suddenly appear in Elizabeth's reign. There had been many in the Middle Ages, but in the sixteenth century their numbers grew (source 50). It is difficult to work out why this happened, but several explanations have been put forward (source 51).

At the end of the previous century Henry VII had passed a law saying that great lords could no longer keep bands of retainers. Many of those who would formerly have enrolled in the service of a lord now led a wandering life (source 52).

ABOVE: A lady spinning

PAGE 42: Four beggars, a contemporary woodcut

SOURCE 50 Some contemporaries wrote as if beggars were a new problem in the sixteenth century

It is not yet full threescore years since this trade [begging] began, but how it hath prospered since that time it is easy to judge, for they are now supposed, of one sex and another, to account unto above 10 000 persons as I have heard reported. Moreover, in counterfeiting the Egyptian rogues, they have devised a language among themselves which they name "canting" but others "pedlars French", a speech compact thirty years since of English and a great number of odd words of their own devising . . . none but themselves are able to understand.

Harrison, *Description of England*, pp. 183-4

SOURCE 51 The causes of poverty

(the numbers in this source refer to a collection of contemporary documents-Tawney and Power, *Tudor Economic Documents*, Vol. III, pp. 452-4)

Pauperism was the result of many factors—rising population, conversion of arable to pasture, enclosure of common lands, racking of rents, growing dependence of industrial producers on overseas markets, the cutting down of great feudal households. An assessment of 1597 gave the causes of poverty and vagabondage as (i) excessive luxury expenditure, leading to racking of rents and sale of lands; (ii) and (ix) excessive consumption of food by the rich, leading to scarcity and high prices; (iii) oppressive landlords; (iv) usury; (v) cornering of corn and holding out for high prices; (vi) wasting of substance at law; (vii) gambling; (viii) breaking up of households, unnecessary dismissals of servants and apprentices; (x) failure to execute the poor law.

Christopher Hill, *Society and Puritanism in Pre-Revolutionary England*, Mercury Books, 1966, p. 262

SOURCE 52 Many beggars were formerly retainers or serving-men of a great lord

The ruffler . . . hath served in the wars, or else he hath been a serving-man; and, weary of well-doing, shaking off all pain, doth choose for himself this idle life and wretchedly wanders about the most shires of this realm.

Thomas Harman, *A Caveat for Common Cursetors*, London, 1567-73, in Edward Viles & F. J. Furnivall (eds.), *The Rogues and Vagabonds of Shakespeare's Youth*, New Shakespeare Society, 1880, p. 29

BELOW: Title page of Thomas Harman's *Caveat for Common Cursetors*

A Caueat or Warening, FOR COMMEN CVRSE-TORS VVLGARELY CALLED Uagabones, set forth by Thomas Harman. Esquiere, for the btilite and p2offyt of his naturall Cuntrey. Augmented and inlarged by the fyst autho2 here of. Anno Domini. M. D. LXVII.

Vewed, examined and allowed, according vnto the Queenes Maiestyes Iniunctions.

Imprinted at London in Fleetstrete at the signe of the Falcon, by Wyllia Gryffith, and are to be sold at his shoppe in Saynt Dunstones Churche parde. in the West. Anno Domini. 1 5 6 7.

Reasons for unemployment

Industry and trade were growing fast. The most important of all was the cloth industry, so when trade with other countries declined for any reason, those areas of the country where cloth making was established were hard hit. The great demand for English cloth made it more profitable for land-owners to breed sheep than to grow crops. In a few areas of the country, mainly in the Midlands, arable land was turned over to grazing. In these areas small farmers and farm labourers were made redundant because fewer men were needed to tend sheep than had previously been employed to grow crops (sources 53, 54).

SOURCE 53 The House of Commons frequently debated the question of the increase in sheep-farming

1597. On Saturday the 5th day of November the House met about eight of the clock in the morning;

Mr Francis Bacon spoke first . . . and made a motion against enclosures and de-population of towns and houses of husbandry and tillage. And to this purpose he brought in, as he termed it, two bills not drawn with a polished pen, but with a polished heart . . .

For enclosure of grounds brings depopulation, which brings first idleness, secondly decay of tillage, thirdly subversion of houses, and decay of charity, and charges to the poor, fourthly impoverishing the state of the Realm.

Mr Bacon did move the house that a committee might be appointed to consider of the said matter touching enclosures.

D'Ewes, *Journal of the Parliaments of Elizabeth*, pp. 551-2

SOURCE 54 The importance of agriculture is illustrated in the preamble to an Act of 1598

And whereas by . . . tillage and husbandry the greater part of the subjects are preserved from extreme poverty in a competent estate of maintenance and means to live, and the wealth of the realm is kept dispersed and distributed in many hands, where it is more ready to answer all necessary charges for the service of the realm; and whereas also the said husbandry and tillage is a cause that the realm doth more stand upon itself, without

BELOW: Various types of beggar

A Soap-eater, copied from a rare print of the time of Queen Elizabeth

A Tom of Bedlam copied from an old Drawing of the time of Edw: 6 in the possession of Franc: Douce Esq.

Copied from a Drawing of the time of Henry VIII in the possession of Francis Douce, Esq.

depending upon foreign countries either for bringing in of corn in time of scarcity, or for vent and utterance of our own commodities being in over-great abundance.

Statutes of the Realm, Vol. IV, p. 893

ABOVE: "Three rows a penny, pins!"

Population growth and rising prices

Throughout the country prices were rising rapidly, far more rapidly than wages. This meant that those who were already poor became even poorer. Many things helped to push prices higher, but one of the most important was a rapid increase in population. With more people to be fed the demand for food increased. It became comparatively scarce and consequently its price began to rise. Those with the least money were the first to be hit by a rise in food prices (sources 55-58).

The increase in population affected the poor in other ways. There were more people looking for work and because the number of jobs did not increase with the number of people, more people were unemployed. Some survived by moving to another place, usually a village or town just a few miles away. Agricultural workers were the hardest hit because their work was seasonal. They went around hiring fairs in different places looking for work, but there was the danger that if they were on the road for too long they would be classed as vagrants.

SOURCE 55 Prices of everyday articles were rising rapidly

Whereas in times past . . . we had sugar for 4 pence that now, at the writing of this treatise, is well worth half-a-crown, raisins or currants for a penny that now are holden at 6 pence, and sometimes at 8 pence and 10 pence the pound, nutmegs at 2½ pence the ounce, ginger at a penny an ounce . . .

Harrison, *Description of England*, p. 116

SOURCE 56 The high price of corn was not always caused by poor harvests

1597, April 30. Hum. Guybon, Sheriff of Norfolk, to Lord Burghley. The daily excess of carriage of corn to port towns, and other places, under colour of its being provision for gentleman's families in other countries [counties], so increases that it is feared that there will not be sufficient to relieve ourselves within our own country [county], and the prices of corn daily rise, being such as were never known before; wheat, 53s 4d per quarter; meslynne, 48s; rye, 46s; barley, 42s; peas and beans, 32s and oats, 24s. The common people grudge the corn being suffered to pass, and at this time, in three several places of the country [county], they have assembled in a very riotous and tumultuous manner, especially at Hatcham, near Lynn, where 24 persons, upon their own authority, stayed a ship laden with corn bound for Gainsborough, and forcibly unloaded her . . .

M. A. E. Green (ed.), *Calendar of State Papers, Domestic, 1595-1597*, London, 1869, p. 401

SOURCE 57 A price index

Perhaps the least inadequate general index of prices is that devised by Professor Phelps Brown and Dr Hopkins, which is based on the cost of the items in the hypothetical weekly budget of a building labourer in southern England. If prices in 1510 are taken as 100, they had risen by 1521 to 167. The index drops slightly to 150 in the early 1540s, and then rises to over 200 in the later 1540s and to 270 in 1555, 370 in 1556, and 409 in 1557, dropping suddenly to 230 in 1558. Since many people were living on a subsistence level in good years, it is not surprising that the late 1550s produced an exceptionally high death rate and unpopular governments. In 1597, a year of disastrously bad harvests, the index rose 180 points in one year to a peak 685, and finally settled down in the early seventeenth century in the area of above 500.

This index gives some picture of a range of price rises which is likely to have caused considerable dismay after a century during which prices had been more or less stable.

Conrad Russell, *The Crisis of Parliaments: English History 1509-1660*, O.U.P., 1971, p. 6

SOURCE 58 The increase in population was noted at the Commission for Almshouses in 1594

That the number of our people is multiplied, it is both demonstrable to the eye and evident in reason, considering on the one side that nowadays not only young folks of all sorts but churchmen also of each degree do marry and multiply at liberty, which was not wont to be, and on the other side that we have not, God be thanked, been touched with any extreme mortality, either by sword or sickness, that might abate the overgrown number of us. And if all, then each sort, and in them the poorer sort also, must needs be augmented.

[In the years immediately after Lambarde wrote this there were three severe famines.]

Read, *William Lambarde and Local Government*, p. 182

ABOVE: A ratcatcher, an illustration from a contemporary ballad sheet

Why were the authorities concerned about the poor?

In theory, until the end of the 1530s the Church, in particular the monasteries, was largely responsible for the poor. In practice the monasteries used only a tiny proportion of their money to help the poor, but they did provide some relief. Many people hoped when they were dissolved in 1539 that some of the money from their sale would be used to provide other forms of help for the poor. The fact that this did not happen, and that the number of vagrants increased, forced the authorities to be aware of the poor (source 59).

The poor, particularly vagrants, were regarded as a problem for two main reasons. Firstly vagrants were suspected, often with good reason, of being criminals, so they were seen as a threat to law and order (source 60). Secondly there was a growing feeling, especially amongst the Puritans, see 'Catholics and Puritans', that idleness was wrong in itself. Everyone should be encouraged to work, and punished if they refuse to do so. There was a growing realization during the reign that a distinction should be made between the poor who could work, but would not, and those who were poor through no fault of their own (source 61).

SOURCE 59 Private charity could not cope with the growing demands

. . . considering your most tender, pitiful, gentle, and noble nature—not only having a vigilant and merciful eye to your poor, indigent and feeble parishioners; yea, not only in the parish where your honour most happily doth dwell, but also in others nearby . . . abundantly pouring out your ardent and bountiful charity upon all such as come for relief unto your gates . . .

'The Epistle to Lady Elizabeth, Countess of Shrewsbury', in Harman, *Caveat for Cursetors*, p. 19

SOURCE 60 Control of vagabonds was closely connected with the maintenance of law and order

1572, Dec 28. York. Articles drawn up by the Council of the North to the justices of the peace. You are first to inquire and certify to us the names and addresses of all known and suspected papists within your rule, the enemies of God and of good order, especially of such as do not come to church. To say the spreading of false and seditious rumours and the sending of messages from the late rebels to trouble the quiet of the realm, order is to be given in market towns and other places, that all suspected passengers, vagabonds, beggars, and rogues be punished with severity and celerity, according to the late statute.

You shall also provide for the relief of the poor, aged and impotent, and certify your proceedings to us within one month.

Green, *State Papers, Domestic, 1566–1579*, p. 435

SOURCE 61 **Different sorts of poor people**

With us the poor is commonly divided into three sorts, so that some are poor by impotency, as the fatherless child, the aged, blind and lame, and the diseased person that is judged to be incurable: the second are poor by casualty, as the wounded soldier, the decayed householder, and the sick person visited with grievous and painful disease: the third consisteth of thriftless poor, as the rioter that hath consumed all, the vagabond that will abide nowhere but runneth up and down from place to place, and finally the rogue and the strumpet.

Harrison, *Description of England*, p. 180

How did the authorities deal with the problem?

It was the towns.which first had to deal with the worst problems of poverty. Many of the unemployed came to the towns in search of work, and the crime rate was much higher as a result.

London
London had already made some provision for the poor. There were St Bartholomew's Hospital for the sick and bedridden, St Thomas's for the aged sick and infirm, Christ's Hospital for orphan children, and Bedlam for the insane. Nicholas Ridley, Bishop of London, had helped to restore St Bartholomew's and St Thomas's in the 1550s because he and many others were

PAGE 48 TOP: Stoneware for sale
PAGE 48 BOTTOM: A ballad singer

BELOW: The Southwark Gate at London Bridge

ABOVE: The brank
BELOW: A beggar being whipped at
the cart's tail

SPECTATUM ADMISSI RI
TENEATIS IMICA

concerned about the fate of the poor in the city (source 62). There were two further problems for the authorities. Poor people from outside the city began coming to London in search of relief because none was provided in their own parishes. It was clear that not all the poor were helpless, some were sturdy vagabonds, fit enough to work, but too lazy to do so. It was believed that they should be punished, partly to teach them how wrong they were, but also to discourage others from following their example. It was usual for them to be publicly disgraced and whipped (source 63). To deal with such vagabonds Edward VI set aside the palace of Bridewell as a 'house of correction' to train them to work. Later, when other towns founded similar institutions, they called them Bridewells.

SOURCE 62 London provides for the poor

Hospitals in this city, and suburbs thereof, that have been of old time, and now presently are, I read of these as followeth.

St Bartholomew's in Smithfield, a hospital of great receipt, and relief for the poor, was suppressed by Henry the eight, and again by him given to the city, and is endowed by the citizens' benevolence . . .

St Thomas's in Southwark being a hospital of great receipt for the poor, was suppressed, but again newly founded and endowed by the benevolence and charity of the citizens of London . . .

Christ's Hospital in Newgate market of a new foundation in the Greyfriars church by King Henry the eight: poor fatherless children be there brought up and nourished at the charges of the citizens, to the number of _____ .

Bridewell, now a hospital (or house of correction) founded by King Edward the sixth, to be a workhouse for the poor and idle persons of the city, wherein a great number of vagrant persons be now set a work and relieved at the charges of the citizens.

John Stow, *A Survey of London*, 1603, Charles L. Kingsford (ed.), Clarendon Press, Vol. II, 1908, pp. 143-5

SOURCE 63 Vagabonds were disgraced and punished in London during the early sixteenth century

29 March, 16 Elizabeth—True Bill that, at Harrowehill co. Middlesex on the said day, John Allen, Elizabeth Turner, Humfrey Foxe, Henry Bower and Agnes Wort, being

over fourteen years old and having no lawful means of livelihood were vagrants and had been vagrants in other parts of the country. Sentenced to be flogged severely and burnt on the right ear.

G.D.R., 26 April, 16 Eliz.

J. C. Jeaffreson (ed.), *Middlesex County Records*, Vol. I, Middlesex County Records Society, 1886, p. 87

Ipswich and Norwich

Ipswich and Norwich were the first to follow London's example. By 1570 there were 2000 beggars in Norwich so some action had to be taken. Both towns established Bridewells and also hospitals for the infirm. They supported the unemployed and devised schemes to provide work for them, mainly in the cloth industry. Surveys were made and genuine beggars were given badges so that people would not be tricked into giving their money away. To pay for poor relief both Norwich and Ipswich levied a compulsory rate (sources 64-74).

SOURCE 64 Norwich sets up a Bridewell in 1571

. . . at the house called the Normans in the convenientist place therefor, shall be appointed a working place, as well as for men as for women viz for the men to be prepared fourteen malt querns to grind malt and such exercises. And for the women to spin and card and such like exercises.

Which working place shall contain to set twelve persons or more upon work which persons shall be kept as prisoners to work for meat and drink for the space of twenty and one days at the least and longer if cause serve and they shall not eat but as they can earn . . .

Which persons shall begin their works at five of the clock in summer viz from Our Lady the Annunciation until Michaelmas and shall end their works at eight of the clock at night, and in winter to begin at six of the clock from Michaelmas to Our Lady, and to end at seven of the clock at night . . .

And those that shall refuse to do their works to them appointed or keep their hours to be punished by the whip.

'The Mayors Book for the Poor: Orders for the Poor 1571,' in Hudson, *Records of Norwich*, pp. 347-8

MULLD·SAKE

ABOVE: John Cottington, chimney sweep and thief

SOURCE 65 The Privy Council commends Norwich for establishing a Bridewell

1579 The Council to the Bishop of Norwich and the Justices of Norfolk. Commend their exertions in the erecting of a form for the punishment of loiterers, stubborn servants, and the setting of vagabonds, rogues and other idle people to work, after the manner of Bridewell.

Green, *State Papers, Domestic*, 1547-1580, p. 462'

SOURCE 66 Norwich makes a census of the poor

These be the names of the poor within the said city as they were viewed in the year of our Lord God 1570. In the time of Mr John Alldrith mayor.

THE WARD OF SOUTH CONSFORTH

NAMES OF THE POOR TO BE REVIEWED WEEKLY IN ST PETERS OF SOUTHGATE

Richard Rich of the age of 35 years, a husbandman which worketh with Mrs Cautrell and keepeth not with his wife (but at times) and helpeth her little. And Margaret his wife of the age of 40 years she spins white warp and Joan her daughter, of the age of 12 years, that spins also the same. And Simond her son of the age of 8 years that goes to school. And Alice and Faith the eldest of the age of 8 years and the other of the age of 3 years . . .

Peter Browne a cobbler of the age of 50 years and hath little work. And Agnes his wife of the age of 52 years that worketh not, but have been sick since Christmas (but in health now) she spins white warp having three daughters, the one of the age of 18 years, the other of the age of 14 years, and the other of the age of 13 years, the which all spin when they can get it, but now they are without work . . .

J. F. Pound (ed.), *The Norwich Census of the Poor 1570*, Vol. XL, Norfolk Record Society, 1971, p.23

SOURCE 67 Ipswich town council orders a survey to be made of the poor within the town boundaries

Wednesday, 2 December 1551. Two in every parish shall be nominated by the Bailiffs to inquire into the poor of every parish, and thereof to make certificate to the Bailiffs.

Nathaniel Bacon, *The Annalls of Ipswiche*, W. H. Richardson (ed.), Ipswich, 1884, p. 235

SOURCE 68 Church collections are to be used for relief of the poor in Ipswich

Friday, June 3. 1552. The Guild shall be holden upon the Sunday after Trinity Sunday, yearly, according to the ancient order: and the communion shall be celebrated at the Tower Church, beginning at 9 of the clock the same day. The Bailiffs, Portmen . . . and the wardens of the several companies, all of them in their several habits or gowns, and they and all the Burgesses shall offer, and the offerings shall go to the poor: the defaulters of the Portmen shall forfeit 12 pence apiece . . . and of the Burgesses 4 pence, unless reasonable cause showed.

Bacon, *Annalls of Ipswiche*, p. 237

SOURCE 69 Beggars in Ipswich must have a licence and wear a badge

Monday, 22 Febr: 1557. No children of this town shall be permitted to beg, and such as shall be admitted thereto shall have badges.

Bacon, *Annalls of Ipswiche*, p. 247

SOURCE 70 Ipswich provides a hospital for the care of poor people

Monday, Septemb: 26. 1569. The late house of Blackfriars, bought of John Southwell Esq shall be henceforth a hospital for the poor people of this town, and shall be called Christ's hospital.

Bacon, *Annalls of Ipswiche*, p. 238

SOURCE 71 Ipswich makes work available for the unemployed

Thursday, 1 April 1591. An order for the clothiers of this town to set poor on work within the town, and if any shall refuse or misuse the work, they shall be punished by the bailiffs.

Bacon, *Annalls of Ipswiche*, p. 365

ABOVE: A beggar

Paremptitius

ABOVE: Women going to market, and an apprentice fetching water

SOURCE 72 **Begging and giving alms were forbidden in Norwich**

Orders for the poor.

1. First that no person or persons old or young shall be suffered to go abroad after a general warning given, or be found a begging in the streets at the sermon or at any man's door or at any place within the city in pain of six stripes with a whip.

2. Not that any person or persons, shall sustain or feed any such beggars at their doors in pain of such fine as is appointed by statute . . .

'The Mayor's Book for the Poor', in Hudson, *Records of Norwich*, p. 347

SOURCE 73 **A regular search is to be made in Norwich for vagabonds**

. . . one officer to go daily about the city, with a staff in his hand to arrest whomsoever is apt for bridewell and bring them to master mayor or to any of the committees . . .

'The Mayor's Book for the Poor', in Hudson, *Records of Norwich*, p. 351

ABOVE: The Almonry, Westminster

SOURCE 74 Norwich makes provision for orphan children and children of poor parents

. . . that there be also appointed . . . so many select women as shall suffice to receive of persons within that ward, viz. of women, maidens or children that shall be appointed unto them . . . to work or learn letters in their house or houses, of the most poorest children whose parents are not able to pay for their learning or of women and maids that live idly or be disordered . . .

The same to be driven to work and learn, by the hours appointed in bridewell and with such corrections, till their hands be brought into such use and their bodies to such pains as labour and learning shall be easier to them than idleness and as they shall of themselves be able to live of their own works with their families as others do.

'The Mayor's Book for the Poor', in Hudson, *Records of Norwich*, pp. 352-3

Poor law reforms

A poor harvest in 1571 led to another period of unrest. Members of Parliament, debating the subject of vagabonds in that year, revealed many shades of opinion. Two Acts, passed in 1572 and 1576, attempted to apply to the whole country the lessons that had been learned from the efforts of the towns. Severe measures were introduced to deal with idle beggars; a compulsory rate was raised for the relief of the poor and houses of correction were to be established to provide work for the unemployed (sources 75-79).

SOURCE 75 The debate in the House of Commons on the Bill against vagabonds, 1571

The Bill against vagabonds was read the first time; after which ensued divers speeches...

Mr Sands endeavoured to prove this Law for Beggars, to be over sharp and bloody, standing much on the care which is to be had for the poor; saying that it might be possible with some travail had by the justices, to relieve every man at his own house and to stay them from wandering; this experience he showed, and what was done in the County of Worcester. Mr Treasurer [Sir Francis Knollys] talked to this effect, that he would have a Bridewell in every town, and every tippler in the country to yield twelve pence yearly to the maintenance thereof.

Mr Wilson a master of the requests, argued thus; that poor of necessity we must have, for so Christ hath said; . . . he said it was no charity, to give to such a one, as we know not, being a stranger unto us.

D'Ewes, *Journal of the Parliaments of Elizabeth*, p. 165

SOURCE 76 A compulsory poor rate is introduced by Parliament in 1572

. . . And when the number of poor people forced to live upon alms be known, the justices, mayors, sheriffs, bailiffs and other officers shall, . . . set down what portion the weekly charge towards the relief of the said poor people will amount unto within their several divisions and limits . . . and shall tax all inhabitants dwelling in every city, borough, town, village, hamlet and place known within the said divisions to such weekly charge as they shall each contribute towards the relief of the said poor people . . .

Statutes of the Realm, Vol. IV, p. 593

SOURCE 77 Parliament enacts that the unemployed shall be provided with work in 1576

. . . to the intent youth may be accustomed and brought up in labour and work, and thus not like to grow idle rogues, and to the intent also that such as be already grown up in idleness and so [be] rogues at this present, may not have any just excuse in saying that they cannot get any service or work . . . and that other poor and needy persons being willing to work may be set on work . . . in every city and town within this realm a store and stock of wool, hemp, flax, iron or other stuff . . . shall be provided.

Collectors and governors of the poor shall deliver to such poor and needy person a portion to be wrought into yarn or other matter . . . for which they shall make payment to them.

Statutes of the Realm, Vol. IV, p. 611

SOURCE 78 The Act against vagabonds is carried out in London

9 June, 17 Elizabeth [1575]—True Bill, that Thomas Maynerde, Oswald Thompson and John Barres (having at the Justice Hall in the Old Bailey, on 18 March 17 Elizabeth [1575], before Sir James Hawes knt. Mayor of London, and William Fleetwood eq. JP, been flogged severely and burnt "per le gristle dextre auricle" [through the right ear]

BELOW: Examples of equipment for punishing beggars

with a hot iron of a thumb's circuit, according to the form of the statute of 14 Elizabeth entitled "An Act for the punishments of vagabonds" . . .) being over eighteen years old, and fit for labour, but masterless and without any lawful means of livelihood, were again on the said day of June wandering as felonious vagrants at St Giles's-in-the-Field and elsewhere in the said county. Putting themselves 'Guilty' without chattels, the three incorrigible vagrants were sentenced to be hung.

Jeaffreson, *Middlesex Records*, p. 94

SOURCE 79 London continues its campaign against vagrants

. . . in the ten weeks between 6 Oct 32 Elizabeth [1590] and 14 Dec. 71 persons, male or female, and aged fourteen or upwards, were sentenced to be severely whipped and branded with a hot iron for being masterless vagrants in the county . . .

Jeaffreson, *Middlesex Records*, p. 191

ABOVE: A persistent beggar is publicly hanged
LEFT: Beggars were severely punished

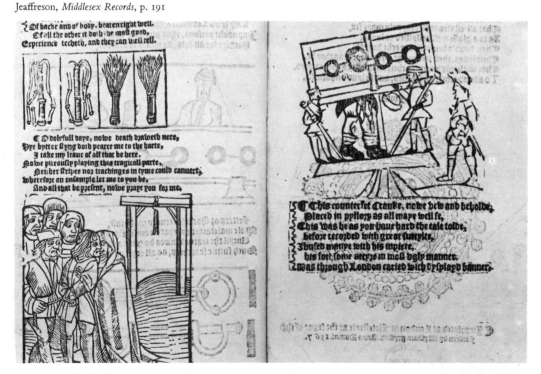

Special measures

Throughout Elizabeth's reign the authorities had tried to overcome the problem of vagrancy by severe punishments. They also began to distinguish more and more carefully between vagrants who were to be punished, and the deserving poor who were to receive relief.

The Privy Council tried in the years following the Acts of 1572 and 1576 to ensure that the regulations were obeyed. There was another bad harvest in 1586 and special measures were taken to ensure that corn was made available to those in need. Organised relief of the poor was then seen to be the most effective way to repress vagrancy.

There was a prolonged period of famine in the years 1594 to 1597. The price of corn rose to four or five times its average in years of good harvest. The unrest in the country led to a new debate in Parliament and a thorough review of the whole question of vagrancy and the poor. Before the session ended, a number of Acts were passed covering every aspect of the question. These laws were renewed in 1601, with minor changes, and they then formed the basis of England's poor laws for more than 200 years (source 80).

SOURCE 80 The Act of 1601, the Poor Law

The poor and impotent persons of every parish shall be relieved of that which every person will of their charity give weekly; and the same relief shall be gathered in every parish by collectors assigned, and weekly distributed to the poor; for none of them shall openly go or sit begging. And if any parishioner shall obstinately refuse to pay reasonably towards the relief of the said poor, or shall discourage others; then the Justices of the Peace at the Quarter Sessions may tax him a reasonable weekly sum; which, if he refuses to pay, they may commit him to prison.

Adapted from the *Statutes of the Realm*, Vol. IV

LEFT: A man and woman in the stocks

4
Catholics and Puritans

When Elizabeth came to the throne it was less than half a century since Martin Luther had made the first break with the Catholic Church in Europe and begun a separate Protestant Church. Most people thought that if a country was to be united and free from civil war all its citizens must believe in the same religion and belong to the same Church (sources 81, 82).

In 1534 Henry VIII had broken away from the Roman Catholic Church and established the Church of England. His daughter, Mary Tudor, became Queen in 1553 and took England back into the Catholic Church, so when Elizabeth became Queen, England was Catholic.

SOURCE 81 In December 1580 Sir William Cecil speaks of religion and treason

. . . there could be no government where there was division. And that state could never be in safety, where there was toleration of two religions. For there is no enmity so great as that for religion. And they that differ in their service of God, can never agree in the service of their country.

F. Peck, *Desiderata Curiosa, or a collection of divers scarce and curious pieces relating chiefly to matters of English history*, London, 1779, p. 33

SOURCE 82 The Earl of Essex agrees with this opinion

. . . where there is no unity in the church there can be no unity or order in the State.

John Strype, *Annals of the Reformation and Establishment of Religion and other Various Occurrences in the Church of England during Queen Elizabeth's Happy Reign*, Vol. I, London, 1725, p. 572

ABOVE: Mary Tudor and Henry VIII

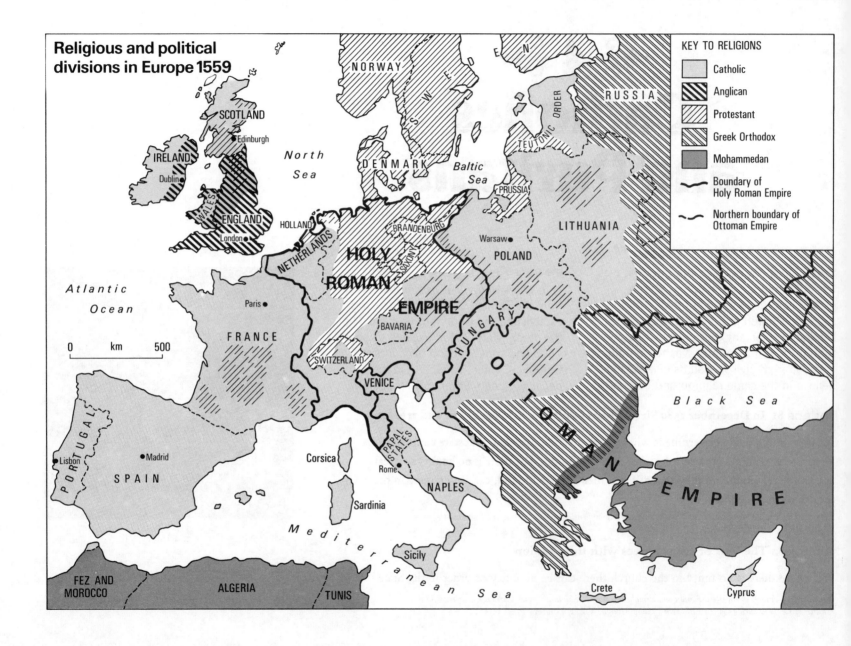

Religious and political divisions in Europe 1559

KEY TO RELIGIONS

- Catholic
- Anglican
- Protestant
- Greek Orthodox
- Mohammedan
- Boundary of Holy Roman Empire
- Northern boundary of Ottoman Empire

NORWAY

SCOTLAND
Edinburgh

IRELAND
Dublin

North Sea

SWEDEN

DENMARK

Baltic Sea

RUSSIA

TEUTONIC ORDER

PRUSSIA

LITHUANIA

WALES
ENGLAND
London

HOLLAND

NETHERLANDS

BRANDENBURG

SAXONY

HOLY ROMAN EMPIRE

BAVARIA

Warsaw

POLAND

Atlantic Ocean

0   km   500

Paris

FRANCE

SWITZERLAND

VENICE

HUNGARY

OTTOMAN

Black Sea

PORTUGAL

Lisbon

Madrid

SPAIN

Corsica

PAPAL STATES

Rome

NAPLES

Sardinia

EMPIRE

Mediterranean Sea

Sicily

Crete

Cyprus

FEZ AND MOROCCO

ALGERIA

TUNIS

Elizabeth's religious settlement

With both Catholic and Protestant subjects Elizabeth aimed to establish a Church which all could attend. In 1559 an Act of Parliament made Elizabeth Supreme Governor of the Church of England, so it was clear that the Church would no longer be Roman Catholic. However, the Act of Uniformity made it law that all church services should be conducted according to *The Book of Common Prayer*. This meant that in many ways services would not be unlike those of the Roman Catholic Church. Elizabeth hoped to make it possible for Catholics and Protestants to worship together, so that the unity of the country would be preserved. Everyone had to attend the Church of England and those who did not go to church on Sundays were fined a shilling a week for recusancy or non-attendance. Not all J.P.s were strict about checking up and collecting the fines (sources 83-88).

TOP: The burning of heretics and heretical literature from Foxe's *Book of Martyrs*
ABOVE: Execution of Catholics in Henry VIII's reign

SOURCE 83 All the Queen's great officers had to swear an Oath of Allegiance

. . . All and every Archbishop, Bishop . . . and all and every temporal Judge, Mayor and other lay or temporal officer . . . shall take an oath . . . that it to say: I A. B. do utterly testify and declare in my conscience, that the Queen's highness is the only supreme Governor of this Realm . . .

Statutes of the Realm, Vol. IV, p. 352

SOURCE 84 It was treason to preach against Elizabeth's supremacy

. . . if any person or persons dwelling or inhabiting within this Realm . . . shall by writing printing teaching preaching express words deed or act . . . [to] defend the authority spiritual or ecclesiastical of any foreign Prince Prelate Person State or Potentate within this Realm . . . the third time shall be deemed and adjudged [guilty of] High Treason and shall suffer pains of death.

Statutes of the Realm, Vol. IV, pp. 353-4

SOURCE 85 Attendance at church was to be made compulsory

. . . all persons shall diligently and faithfully . . . endeavour themselves to resort to their parish church or chapel accustomed . . . upon every Sunday and other days ordained and to be used as Holy Days . . . upon pain that every person so offending shall forfeit for every such offence twelve pence, to be levied by the Churchwardens of the parish where such offence shall be done, to the use of the poor of the same parish . . .

Statutes of the Realm, Vol. IV, pp. 356-7

BELOW: Elizabeth I going in procession to St. Paul's Cathedral

SOURCE 86 Everyone must worship according to *The Book of Common Prayer*

. . . all and singular Ministers in any cathedral or parish church . . . shall be bound to say Matins, Evensong, Celebration of the Lord's Supper . . . and all their common and open prayer in such order and form as is mentioned in the Book authorised by Parliament . . .

Statutes of the Realm, Vol. IV, pp. 355-6

SOURCE 87 The variations in the service and the dress of ministers

Service and Prayer.

Some say the service and prayers in the chancel; others in the body of the church; some in the pulpit with their faces to the people. Some keep precisely the order of the book [of common prayer]; others intermeddle Psalms in metre. Some say with a surplice; others without a surplice.

John Strype, *The Life and Acts of Matthew Parker, The First Archbishop in the Reign of Queen Elizabeth*, Oxford, 1821, p. 302

SOURCE 88 The report from the Archbishop of York to the Privy Council in 1564 about the Justices of the Peace

The Certificate of Thomas Archbishop of York to the right honourable the Lords and others of the Queen's Majesty's most honourable Privy Council. Touching and concerning their letters for Justices of Peace within the County of York . . .

West Riding:

Thomas Gargrave, John York, Richard Corbett, George Browne, Henry Savill . . . Justices that be favourers of religion.

William Vavasour, William Ingleby, Thomas Danby, William Mallary, Francis Woodroff . . .

Justices that be no favourers.

'Letters from the Bishop to the Privy Council,' 1564, in *Camden Miscellany*, Vol. 9, Camden Society, 1895, p. 70

Reactions to the settlement

In some ways Elizabeth was fortunate. Many of the bishoprics were vacant and the Catholic Archbishop of Canterbury appointed by Mary died soon after she did. The remaining bishops (except one) refused to serve in the new Church so Elizabeth could make new appointments. She had to appoint men who had been exiles in Mary's reign and many of them were more Protestant than she would have wished. The most important appointment was given to Matthew Parker who became Archbishop of Canterbury. He was a scholar, a moderate, and a close friend of Cecil. He was not the man to give the lead to the exiles who wanted to make the Church of England more like the Protestant churches of Europe.

Elizabeth's hopes that everyone would accept her religious settlement were quickly dashed. In 1564 the Archbishop of Canterbury reported that many ministers were ignoring the instructions in *The Book of Common Prayer*. In the same year the Privy Council carried out an investigation into the religious opinions of the J.P.s. The result of the investigation showed that: 431 were favourable to the Church of England; 157 were definitely not favourable to the

Church of England and 264 were neutral or not favourable.

At first it seemed that the Catholics posed a more serious threat than the extreme Protestants to the peace of the kingdom.

The Catholics 1559-1567

Elizabeth's very position as Queen of England was challenged by the Catholics who believed that Mary, Queen of Scots had a better claim to the throne. In 1561 Mary had returned to Scotland from France after the death of her husband, Francis II, so she was close at hand to threaten Elizabeth. Scotland had by then become a Protestant country, so Mary could not hope for as much support from the Scottish nobility as she might have had earlier in the reign. The death of her husband also meant that she would be unlikely to get support from the French government.

France, as a Catholic country, might well have been a threat to England, but in 1562 trouble between Catholics and Protestants there broke into civil war. With trouble inside her own borders, France was un-

ABOVE: Matthew Parker, Archbishop of Canterbury

likely to want to fight against England. Although Elizabeth sent some help to the French Protestants, she was very discreet about this, and careful not to provoke France into war against England.

Another country which might have turned against England was Spain. Its King, Philip II, was an ardent Catholic and was anxious to stop Protestantism spreading. He felt he had more to gain by being friendly towards Elizabeth, being hopeful at the beginning of her reign that she would marry him. Elizabeth's church settlement was vague enough for him to hope that in the end England might turn Catholic. The Pope seemed to take the same view, and England was left in peace.

1568-1588

By the end of the 1560s Elizabeth was in danger once more. In 1568 Mary, Queen of Scots fled to England, see 'Mary, Queen of Scots: A case study'. A revolt broke out in support of her and the rebels sought help from Philip II of Spain (sources 89, 90).

In 1570 the new Pope, Pius V, was determined to win back Protestant areas of Europe to Catholicism and he excommunicated Elizabeth (source 91). This meant that she was expelled from the Church. Her subjects were not supposed to recognize her as Queen, and indeed should do all they could to find and support a Catholic successor. This ruling from the Pope meant nothing to most of Elizabeth's subjects, but it put the Catholics in a difficult position because their loyalty might now be divided between the Queen and the Pope. Many of those who felt certain that their first loyalty was to the Pope went into exile in Europe, usually to Flanders or Italy.

ABOVE: Philip II of Spain, a portrait by Titian

SOURCE 89 The Spanish Ambassador describes the plot to set Mary, Queen of Scots on the English throne

22 Sept. 1569 . . . a servant of the duke of Northumberland, whom I knew, came to me and made me the sign which his master and I had agreed upon. He said that his Lord and his friends in the North had agreed to liberate the Queen of Scotland, as, thereby, they would assure the Catholic religion, and return to amity and alliance with your Majesty [Philip II of Spain], which they so much desire.

Hume, *State Papers, Spanish*, Vol. II, p. 195

SOURCE 90 The rebels seek help from King Philip II of Spain

8 Oct. 1569 . . . They have sent Northumberland's servant, who spoke to me before on the matter, to say that they will by armed force release the Queen [Mary, Queen of Scots] and take possession of all the north country, restoring the Catholic religion in this country . . . They only ask that, after they have released the Queen, they should be aided by your majesty with a small number of harquebussiers.

Hume, *State Papers, Spanish*, Vol II, p. 199

SOURCE 91 The Pope excommunicates Elizabeth

We do declare the aforesaid Elizabeth . . . to have incurred the sentence of excommunication, and to be cut off from the unity of the Body of Christ. And moreover we do declare her to be deprived of her pretended title to the kingdom . . . And we do command and charge all and every the noblemen, subjects, people, and others aforesaid that they presume not to obey her or her orders, mandates, and laws . . .

William Camden, *The History of the Most Renowned and Victorious Princess Elizabeth, Late Queen of England*, 1615, London, 1688, p. 147

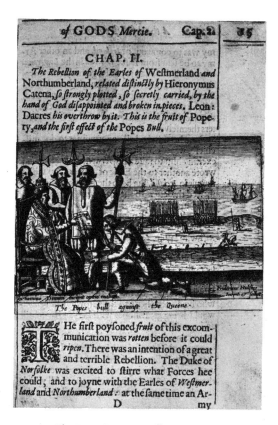

ABOVE: The Pope issues a Bull excommunicating Elizabeth I

A change of policy

From Elizabeth's point of view a Catholic subject was likely to be a traitor. She replied to this ruling from the Pope by a campaign to search out the Catholics, though she was tolerant towards most of the Catholic gentry and nobility (source 92). The treason laws were strengthened, but they would probably have been far more severe if M.P.s had known then about the Ridolfi Plot. Elizabeth, Cecil and Walsingham were just beginning to find out the details of this plot, in which the Pope and Philip II were involved in a plan to overthrow Elizabeth and put Mary, Queen of Scots on the English throne. Commissioners were repeatedly sent around the country to question any who were suspected of being disloyal to Elizabeth. Despite the danger that they might be martyred for their faith, many people continued to worship as Catholics. On 25 May 1570 John Felton died; he was regarded by the Catholics as the first martyr, by the Protestants as a traitor (sources 93-95).

In 1572 there was a passionate feeling in England against the Roman Catholics when news came from France of a massacre of Protestants on St Bartholomew's Day. Thousands were killed in Paris and thousands more in the provinces. What made the killings even more sinister to English Protestants was that it was clear that the Pope approved of the massacre..

SOURCE 92 Elizabeth's tolerance of Catholic gentry

Even after 1569, northern magistrates were reluctant to act against neighbours and friends. Earnest Protestants were happy to do so, but there were few of them in the North, and imported strangers made themselves thoroughly unpopular. Fines were evaded or remained unpaid; the worst offenders were often women, who had no property to be seized.

Elizabeth was not unduly disturbed by these Catholic survivals, so long as they centred round the gentry. In some ways she assisted the process. By her desire, Catholic peers were excused the oath. She did not, on the whole, give them public employment, but she liked to have them at court. In some ways she regarded Catholic peers as supporters of her throne, a balancing factor against the aggressive Protestantism of men like Huntingdon, Bedford and Warwick . . . . Sometimes she visited the houses of known Catholics.

Johnson, *Elizabeth: A study*, pp. 341-2

SOURCE 93 Elizabeth enforces the Act of Uniformity. more strictly

28 Nov. 1574. The Queen has appointed commissioners who are furiously examining the principal Catholics, bishops, and others . . . the substance of their examination being as follows.

If they recognise the Queen as head of the Church of England. To this they have all replied to the same effect, although examined separately, that they did not, and that the Supreme Pontiff [the Pope] is the head of the Universal Church and the vicar of our Lord Jesus Christ. They were then asked if they recognised the Queen as sovereign, to which they replied that they did.

. . . They were then asked if the service in use in churches here, by order of the Queen was acceptable to God, and they distinctly replied that it was not, as it was performed outside the unity of the Church, and contrary to its sacred doctrine. To all these things they, being all Catholics, answered similarly, being ready to live or die in the truth, which they held before men, constant unto martyrdom. Each one had to sign his name to his confession for the information of the Queen and Council. People expect that severity will come of this.

Hume, *State Papers, Spanish*, Vol. II, pp. 488-9

SOURCE 94 Parliament resumes the campaign against the Catholics

18 Feb. 1576. They [Parliament] have agreed already to a great persecution of the Catholics, who will not attend their churches, and have appointed a commissioner to proceed against them in person and estate.

Hume, *State Papers, Spanish,* Vol. II, pp. 525-6

SOURCE 95 People continue to worship as Catholics in spite of the dangers

31 March, 1578. From what I understand, God has been pleased still to maintain some Catholics in this country, and I am told that many persons openly observe the religion, notwithstanding the penalties against it.

They have been much encouraged by an event that happened this summer at Oxford, which was foretold by one of the men whom the judges sentenced to martyrdom three days before it happened.

Hume, *State Papers, Spanish,* Vol. II, p. 572

BELOW: Father Parsons and Father Campion

Catholic missions to England

Meanwhile, many of the English Catholics who had gone into exile were training to be priests, so that they could come back to serve the Catholics who had stayed in England. In 1568 William Allen founded the English College at Douai. Later the English Seminary in Rome was taken over by the Jesuits and became known as the English College (source 96).

Although political discussion was forbidden amongst the students at Douai, Elizabeth and her Council suspected that they intended to overthrow her and put Mary, Queen of Scots on the throne of England. They certainly knew about the training of priests for missions to England because Walsingham had sent spies all over Europe.

ABOVE: William Parry, a Catholic, was hanged for attempting to kill Elizabeth

His informers were so efficient that when, in 1580, a group of fourteen missionaries crossed to England, the Channel ports were watched by men who had full descriptions of the party. Nevertheless, the two chief members, Father Edmund Campion and Father Robert Parsons, got through the net and began their mission as priests in England (source 97).

In the following year Parliament tightened the laws against Roman Catholics. Recusancy fines (for non-attendance at church) were raised from one shilling a week to £20 a month and a fine of £66 was imposed for hearing Mass. Anyone knowingly harbouring a priest or Jesuit was guilty of treason (sources 98,99).

SOURCE 96 Catholic missionaries from abroad begin their work in England

28 Dec. 1579. The number of Catholics, thank God, is daily increasing here, owing to the College and Seminary for Englishmen which your Majesty [Philip II] ordered to be supported in Douai, whence there was come in the last year (and from the College of Rome) a hundred Englishmen who have been ordained there, by which means a great number of people are being converted, generally persons who have never heard the truth preached before. These priests go about disguised as laymen, and although they are young men, their good life, fervency, and zeal in the work are admirable.
Hume, *State Papers, Spanish*, Vol. II, pp. 710-11

SOURCE 97 Anxiety at the arrival of the Jesuits in England

There were numerous disturbing portents recorded on the eve of the Jesuits' arrival. In April the great bell of Westminster tolled of itself without human agency. In June there were thunderstorms of exceptional violence. A woman named Alice Perin, at the age of 80 years, gave birth to a prodigy with a head like a helmet, a face like a man, a mouth like a mouse, a human body, eight legs, all different, and a tail half a yard long, while in the same year another monster was reported from Stowe that was both male and female, with mouth and eyes like a lion. In May a pack of hounds was clearly visible, hunting in the clouds over Wiltshire, while over the border in Somerset three several companies of sixty men each, dressed in black, marched in procession through the sky. Cecil, Elizabeth, and most of the Court took serious notice of auguries and the events caused great anxiety for the government's security.
Evelyn Waugh, *Edmund Campion*, Penguin, 1953, pp. 85-6

SOURCE 98 The Government increases the penalties for not conforming

. . . every person which shall say or sing mass . . . shall forfeit the sum of two hundred marks and be committed to prison in the next gaol, there to remain by the space of one year . . .

. . . every person above the age of 16 years which shall not repair to some church, chapel, or usual place of common prayer, . . . shall forfeit to the Queen's Majesty for every month . . . twenty pounds of lawful English money.

Statutes of the Realm, Vol. IV, p. 657

SOURCE 99 The increased penalties against Roman Catholics, described by a modern Catholic writer

This clause is notable because it is the first time that the Mass is specifically proscribed. Hitherto the offence had been 'to sing or say any common or open prayer or to minister any sacrament otherwise than is mentioned in the said book' [*The Book of Common Prayer*] . . . The object of this legislation was to outlaw and ruin the Catholic community.

Waugh, *Campion*, p. 88

Campion and other Catholic priests

It was dangerous to be a Catholic, and certainly to be a priest. Those, like Campion and Parsons, who travelled around the country, had to be very careful (source 100). They usually stayed in the houses of rich gentry, where there was room for people to come to hear Mass, and where they could hide. Many such houses had 'priest holes', which were specially constructed hiding places; sometimes a hidden room with a secret door, sometimes a simpler and far more cramped hiding place.

It was while he was hiding in a house after saying Mass that Edmund Campion was caught in 1581. He was one of the most saintly of the missionaries to come to England and few seriously thought that he intended to overthrow the Queen (source 101). However his work was considered a threat to the security of the country and at his trial he was found guilty of treason and sentenced to death. Three jurymen had refused to serve at his trial and at his execution there was enormous sympathy from the crowd (sources 102-108).

SOURCE 100 The beginning of Campion's mission

Campion made the aquaintance of the chief Catholics and Catholic sympathizers in London. On the Feast of St. Peter and St. Paul, 29 June, he preached on the historic text 'Tu es Petrus' [You are Peter] before a large audience in the hall of Lord Norreys' house, hired for the occasion by Lord Paget, and daily interviewed a great number who came to him for advice. There seems to have been a friend or agent in Court, for he was successfully protected from the informers who attempted to get access to him in the guise of penitents, among the most dangerous of whom was one Sledd, who had been a servant in Rome and knew by sight many of the missionaries.

Waugh, *Campion*, pp. 93-4

SOURCE 101 Campion's own description of his mission

[It was] in brief, to crie alarme spiritual against foul vice and proud ignorance, where-with many my dear Countrymen are abused.

I never had mind, and am strictly forbidden by our Father that sent me, to deal in any respect with matter of State or Policy of this Realm, as things which appertain not to my vocation, and from which I do gladly restrain and sequester my thoughts.

Waugh, *Campion*, p. 101

SOURCE 102 Campion is captured and tortured

12 Aug. 1581. In accordance with the laws which I said had been passed in this parliament, they have now begun to persecute the Catholics worse than ever before, both by condemning them to the £20 fine if they do not attend church every month and by imprisoning them closely in the goals. The clergymen they succeed in capturing are treated with a variety of terrible tortures: amongst others is one torment that people in Spain imagine to be that which will be worked by Anti-Christ as the most dreadfully cruel of them all. This is to drive iron spikes between the nails and the quick; and two clergymen in the tower have been tortured in this way, one of them being Campion of the Company of Jesus, who, with the other was recently captured. I am assured that when they would not confess under this torture the nails of their

fingers and toes were turned back; all of which they suffered with great patience and humility.

Hume, *State Papers, Spanish*, Vol. III, pp. 152–3

SOURCE 103 An account of the severity of Campion's torture

7 Nov. 1581. After having again terribly tormented Campion, of the Company of Jesus, they have indicted him, as they call it here, as a traitor, with sixteen others,

mostly clergymen. They are in prison, and it is to be feared they will be executed, Campion not yet having been brought to trial, as he is all dislocated and cannot move.

Hume, *State Papers, Spanish*, Vol. III, p. 21

SOURCE 104 Another account of Father Campion's torture

[The Inquisitors] protested: "That the Priests were more favourably dealt with all than they deserved: That they were never once questioned for their Religion, but only for dangerous contrivances against their Prince and Country . . . That Campion was never racked so but that he was presently able to walk, and subscribe his confession".

William Camden, *The History of the Most Renowned and Victorious Princess Elizabeth late Queen of England: Selected Chapters*, W. T. MacCaffrey (ed.), University of Chicago Press, p. 172

SOURCE 105 Elizabeth was reluctant to take stern measures

. . . the Queen (who never was of opinion that men's consciences were to be forced) complained many times that she was driven of necessity to take courses, unless she would suffer the ruin of herself and her subjects, upon some men's pretence of conscience and the Catholic religion.

Camden, *History of Princess Elizabeth*, MacCaffrey, p. 139

SOURCE 106 A description of Campion's execution

They called to him to pray in English, but he replied with great mildness that 'he would pray God in a language which they both well understood'.

There was more noise; the Councillors demanded that he should ask the Queen's forgiveness.

'Wherein have I offended her? In this I am innocent. This is my last speech; in this give me credit—I have and do pray for her'.

Still the courtiers were not satisfied. Lord Howard demanded to know what Queen he prayed for.

'Yea, for Elizabeth your Queen and my Queen, unto whom I wish a long and quiet reign with all prosperity'.

The cart was then driven from under him, the eager crowd swayed forward, and Campion was left hanging, until, unconscious, perhaps already dead, he was cut down and the butcher began his work.

Waugh, *Campion*, pp. 165-6

SOURCE 107 The government claims that Campion was executed for treason

4 Dec. 1581. Knollys, the Treasurer of the Household and a councillor, who is a great heretic, was present at the execution, [of Campion] and cried out that this was not a case of religion, but of treason . . .

Hume, *State Papers, Spanish*, Vol. III, p. 231

SOURCE 108 Another justification for Campion's execution for treason

For Campion, after he was condemned, being asked, first, whether Queen Elizabeth were a right and lawful Queen, refused to answer: then whether he would take part with the Queen, or the Pope if he should send forces against the Queen, he openly professed and testified under his hand that he would stand for the Pope.

Camden, *History of Princess Elizabeth*, MacCaffrey, p. 139

The threat of invasion

The danger to Elizabeth's throne reached a climax in the 1580s. Priests continued to arrive from abroad, and ordinary men and women showed that they were prepared to take unprecedented risks for their faith. When Mary, Queen of Scots was executed in 1587 the leading English Catholics appealed to Philip II of Spain. They wanted him to invade England and win the country back for the Catholic faith (sources 109–111).

Philip prepared a large invasion force, the 'invincible' Armada. He wrote to the Spanish Ambassador in Rome, instructing him to obtain a promise of support from

BELOW: The Spanish Armada being attacked by the English Fleet

the Pope. After many delays the fleet set sail.

The invasion attempt failed and the fleet was destroyed, partly by the small ships of the English navy, and partly by the storms that wrecked the Spanish ships as they fled round the north coast of Scotland. England was saved and there was general public rejoicing. Elizabeth held a service of thanksgiving in St Paul's Cathedral to show that the victory had been achieved by God's blessing (sources 112-116).

SOURCE 109 Men and women were prepared to die for their faith

12 Aug. 1581. At the end of the last month they martyred a clergyman who would not acknowledge the Queen as head of the church . . . He died with invincible constancy and fortitude, greatly to the edification of the Catholics, and the surprise of the heretics themselves. The great number of Catholics there are and their fervent zeal are proved by the fact that two days after his martyrdom there was not a bit of ground left which had been touched by his blood, it having all been taken by the faithful, who also offered large sums of money for his garments.

Hume, *State Papers, Spanish*, Vol. III, p. 153

SOURCE 110 The Privy Council instructs the Justices of the Peace to investigate a suspected Papist

6 September 1586. A letter to Thomas Parry, Read Stafford, and Humfrey Foister, esquires, Justices of the Peace in the county of Berks, signifying the receipt of their letter and information given against Francis Parkins esquire, and divers of his servants, yielding them thanks therefore, and further requiring and authorising them to make repair unto the house of the said Parkins, and to apprehend such of his servants as are named in the Information, whom they are to examine as well by the lewd speeches alleged to be uttered by them or their master, as of the person supposed to be a Priest, or a Seminary . . . committing them to some prison until they shall hear further from their Lordships . . . their Lordships think it requisite likewise that they make search in that place where Mass is suspected to be said, and in his study or other places where his writings are, wherein if they shall find anything whereby he may be further charged, they are likewise to send them hither . . .

Dasent, *Acts of the Privy Council*, Vol. XIV, p. 215

SOURCE 111 An English Catholic in exile, William Allen, writes to urge Philip II to invade England

19 March 1587. Exhorts him to undertake the enterprise against England, his unhappy country. The Catholics are all clamouring for him, and he urges him to crown his glorious efforts in the holy cause of Christ by punishing this woman [Elizabeth] hated of God and man, and restoring the country to its ancient glory and liberty.

Hume, *State Papers, Spanish*, Vol. IV, p. 41

SOURCE 112 In a letter to his Ambassador in Rome, Philip II of Spain indicates his plans to invade England with the support of the Pope

11 February 1587. You will cautiously approach his Holiness [the Pope] and in such terms as you think fit endeavour to obtain from him a secret brief declaring that, failing the Queen of Scotland, the right to the English Crown falls to me . . . You will impress upon his Holiness that I cannot undertake a war in England for the purpose merely of placing upon that throne a young heretic like the king of Scotland [James VI] who, indeed, is by his heresy incapacitated to succeed. His Holiness must, however, be assured that I have no intention of adding England to my own dominions, but to settle the crown upon my daughter, the Infanta.

Hume, *State Papers, Spanish*, Vol. IV, p. 16

SOURCE 113 Philip II insists on financial as well as spiritual aid from the Pope

24 June 1587 . . . it would be well for his Holiness at the time of the execution [of the invasion] to grant a jubilee for those who take part in it, and those who pray for the success of so just and holy a cause . . .

It is also very desirable that you should now ensure the payment of the million, and its anticipation in the form I wrote on the 7th April. This should be done with all possible speed and certainly, without pledging me to any fixed time, although you should say that you are sure I shall carry out the enterprise as soon as I can out of regard to the service of the Lord, the obligations imposed upon us all by the death of the Queen of Scotland, and the saintly wishes of his Holiness.

Hume, *State Papers, Spanish*, Vol. IV, p. 112

ABOVE: A chart showing the course of the battle against the Spanish Armada

SOURCE 114 Elizabeth's advisers tell her that the real danger comes from the Catholics in England

In this troublesome season, some beat it many times into the Queen's head, that the Spaniards abroad were not so much to be feared as the Papists at home; for the Spaniards would not attempt any hostility against England but upon confidence of help from them: and that therefore, for better security, the heads of that party were upon some pretence or other to be taken off . . . But the queen, disliking this as cruel council, thought it sufficient to commit some of the Papists, and those not of the Chief, to custody at Wisbech in the Fens.

Camden, *History of Princess Elizabeth*, MacCaffrey, p. 313

SOURCE 115 The Spanish Armada is destroyed

And thus this great Armada, which had been three complete years in rigging and pre-paring with infinite expense, was within one month's space many times fought with, and at the last overthrown, with the slaughter of many men, not a hundred of the English being missing, nor any ship lost, save only that small one of Cock's: (for all the shot from the tall Spanish ships flew quite over the English): and after it had been driven round about all Britain, by Scotland, the Orcades and Ireland, grievously tossed, and very much distressed, impaired and mangled by storms and wrecks, and endured all manner of miseries, at length returned home with shame and dishonour.

Camden, *History of Princess Elizabeth*, MacCaffrey, pp. 326-7

SOURCE 116 Elizabeth and her people thank God for their great victory

Queen Elizabeth . . . commanded public prayers and thanksgiving to be used through-out all the Churches of England: and she herself, as it were going in triumph, went with a very gallant train of noblemen through the streets of London, which were all hung with blue cloth . . . being carried in a chariot drawn with two horses, (for coaches were not then so much in use amongst princes as now they are amongst private men), to Paul's Church (where the banners taken from the enemy were hung up to be seen), gave most hearty thanks to God, and heard a sermon, wherein the glory was given to God alone.

Camden, *History of Princess Elizabeth*, MacCaffrey, p. 328

After 1588

Although they had rejoiced at the defeat of the Armada, people at the time were not convinced the danger was over. In 1591 commissioners were sent into all parts of the country to enquire about the state of religion. The reports showed that there was still a widespread refusal to conform and in 1593 Parliament passed another law against the Catholics, but the Government experienced great difficulty in enforcing the law (sources 117-120).

SOURCE 117 The commission reports on the state of religion in Lancashire and Cheshire

1591. Report to the Council, on the condition of Lancashire and Cheshire. Small reformation has been made there . . . as may appear by the emptiness of churches on Sundays and holidays . . . The people lack instruction, for the preachers are few, most of the parsons unlearned . . . The youth are for the most part trained up by such as profess papistry; no examination is had of schools and schoolmasters. The proclamation for the apprehension of seminaries, Jesuits and mass priests . . . is not executed . . . the people who resort to church are so few that preachers who were determined to preach on Sundays and holidays have refrained, for lack of auditors; the people so swarm the streets and alehouses during service time, that many churches have only present the curate and his clerk, and open markets are kept in service time.

Green, *State Papers, Domestic*, 1591-1594, p. 158

SOURCE 118 Parliament tightens the law against Catholics

. . . every person above the age of sixteen years . . . being a Popish recusant shall repair to their places of dwelling . . . and shall not any time after pass or remove above five miles from thence . . .

. . . if any person which shall be suspected to be a Jesuit seminary or massing priest . . . shall refuse to answer directly and truly whether he be a Jesuit or a seminary or massing priest . . . shall for his disobedience and contempt in that behalf be committed to prison . . .

Statutes of the Realm, Vol. IV, pp. 843, 845

SOURCE 119 A letter from the Bishop of Chester to Thomas Kesketh shows that the law was not carefully observed

Jan. 29 1598. I hear that the prison at Lancaster is very ill kept; that the recusants there have liberty to go when and whither they list; to hunt, hawk, and go to horse races at their pleasure . . .

Green, *State Papers, Domestic*, 1589-1601, p. 14

SOURCE 120 **The Queen orders Lord Burghley to take stern measures**

3 Aug. 1599. Instructions from the Queen to Lord Burghley, on his appointment to the office of Lord President of York . . .

2. You must reform and correct that abundant falling away from religion, and stir up the Ecclesiastical Commissioners . . . It appears that within the last five or six years, whole parishes have grown recusant, not six households within six miles being found obedient . . . Through toleration and negligence, wilful Papists are unpunished, and authority abused. Dangerous recusants, as Fenton, Danby, Jackson, and Helsthropp, being committed, have been liberated by high commission . . .

Green, *State Papers, Domestic,* 1598-1601, pp. 275-6

The Puritans

The danger from the Puritans was rather different. They did not challenge Elizabeth's claim to the throne, and they could not be accused of working for a foreign power. They did, however, have links with other countries. Many of their leaders had been in exile during Mary Tudor's reign and had been strongly influenced by European Protestants. The churches where they had worshipped in Europe were even less similar to the Catholic Church than the Church of England.

Their name comes from the fact that they wanted to purify the Church of England. They were people who studied the Bible closely and who wanted to return to the simple way of life which had been led by the early Christians. They did not like using *The Book of Common Prayer,* or seeing their ministers dress like Catholic priests. They disliked ceremony and ritual, and indeed anything that reminded them of Catholicism (sources 121-123).

BELOW: A Puritan family

SOURCE 121 **Some Puritan suggestions for reform of the Church of England were made in the Articles of Convocation in 1563**

I. That all Sundays in the year and principal feasts of Christ be kept holy days; and all other holy days to be abrogated.

II. That in all parish churches the minister in common prayer turn his face towards the people; and there distinctly read the divine service appointed where all the people assembled may hear and be edified.

ABOVE: John Goodwin, a Puritan

III. That in ministering the sacrament of baptism, the ceremony of making the cross in the child's forehead may be omitted as tending to superstitions.

IV. That the use of organs be removed.

Strype, *Annals of the Reformation*, Vol. I, p. 337

SOURCE 122 The Puritans attack the Church of England for being too close to the Catholic Church

Coleman, Button, Hallingham, Benson, and others . . . professing a more sincere religion, allowed nothing but what was drawn from the fountains of the Holy Scriptures . . . openly called in question the received discipline of the Church of England, the liturgy, and the vocation of bishops, yea condemned them as favouring too much of the Romish religion . . . using all the means they could, that all things in the Church of England might be reformed according to the pattern of the Church of Geneva. These men though the Queen commanded to be committed to prison, yet incredible it is how much the followers increased everywhere . . . [and] began presently to be known by the odious name of Puritans.

Camden, *History of the Princess Elizabeth*, MacCaffrey, pp. 85-6

SOURCE 123 Puritan beliefs continued to gain a hold

16 July 1583. The sect of Puritans is greatly increasing here, and many of the principal people belong to it. Six gentlemen of the County of Suffolk seeing that the Queen will not reform (as they call it) religion here by killing all the Catholics, have written to members of their sect in France, whom they call 'bretheren', asking their opinion as to whether they were justified in taking up arms against the Queen in deposing her, placing some other in her place, or killing her, in order that their religion might be settled . . . some of the members of the Council were in favour of punishing these men, but as Leicester, Walsingham and Bedford are touched with the same opinions and are friendly with the leaders, they prevented it.

Hume, *State Papers, Spanish*, Vol. III, p. 496

Different types of Puritan

The Puritans were not such a distinct group as the Catholics. The name was often used to describe different kinds of people. One contemporary, Henry Parker, distinguished between four different types: Puritans in religion; Puritans in church policy; Puritans in state; and Puritans in morality.

The first group, the Puritans in religion, are those described above, who wanted to 'purify' the Church of England. Puritans in church policy wanted to go further than this. One of their leaders was John Field, who believed the Puritans should take over the government of the Church of England, and replace the existing system with a Presbyterian one.
This meant changing the structure of the Church. Instead of a hierarchy of bishops deciding Church teachings and practices, there would be a series of meetings and conferences where these matters would be discussed (source 124).

One way in which the Puritans in religion and church policy could spread their ideas was by preaching and lecturing. Preaching was very influential in the sixteenth century, not just because nearly everybody went to church, but also because sermons were often used to tell people about government policy and decisions. Men had to have special licences to preach or to lecture, so Puritans were anxious to have as many licensed

preachers as possible (sources 125, 126). They also held classes and conferences, the best known of which was the London Presbyterian Conference in the 1570s.

The terms Puritans in state and Puritans in morality were used far more loosely. Puritans in morality were probably the most generally unpopular. They were the people who disapproved of dancing and the theatre and frowned on people dressing up and enjoying themselves. There are several references in literature which show that these people were ridiculed and disliked (source 127). Puritans in state usually referred to anyone who opposed the most influential group in the Privy Council at the time. For instance, Leicester and his friends were sometimes called Puritans when they opposed Cecil (source 128).

E. F.

ABOVE: The descent of the Pope into hell

SOURCE 124 A Puritan attack on the bishops of the Church of England

As England was at this time [1588] troubled with enemies abroad, as it was pestered this year also with schism at home: (for schism usually springeth up most rankly in the heat of war) . . . For when the Queen (who was always the same) would not give ear to innovators in religion, who designed (as she thought) to cut in sunder the very sinews of the ecclesiastical government and her royal prerogative at once, some of those men who were great admirers of the discipline of the Church of Geneva thought there was no better way to be taken for establishing the same in England, than by . . . stirring up the people to a dislike and hatred of the bishops and prelacy. These men therefore set forth scandalous books against both the Church-government and the prelates, the titles whereof were Martin Marprelate . . . the authors thereof [were] Penry and Udal, ministers of the Word, and Job Throckmorton, a learned man . . . the said knights [would have] smarted by a heavy fine laid upon them in the Star Chamber, had not the Archbishop of Canterbury (such was his mildness and good nature) with much ado requested and obtained a remission thereof from the Queen.

Camden, *History of the Princess Elizabeth*, MacCaffrey, pp. 331-2

SOURCE 125 The Earl of Leicester defends his patronage of the Puritans in a letter to Thomas Wood written on 17 August 1576

Who in England hath had or hath more learned chapleyns belonging to him than I, or hath preferred more to the furtherance of the Church of learned preachers? . . . And where have I refused any one preacher or good minister to doe for him the best I could at all times, when they have need of me either to speake or write for them?

P. Collinson (ed.), *Letters of Thomas Wood, Puritan, 1566-1577*, Bulletin of the Institute of Historical Research, Special Supplement No. 5, November, 1960, p. 13

SOURCE 126 A sermon preached by Henry Smith in 1590 at St. Clement's in the Strand; an example of Puritan preaching

Who can express that man's horror but himself? Sorrows are met in his soul at a feast: and fear, thought, and anguish divide his soul between them. All the furies of hell leap upon his heart like a stag. Thought calls to Fear; Fear whistles to Horror,

Horror beckons to Despair, and says, come and help me to torment the sinner . . .
Thus he lies upon the rack, and says that he bears the world upon his shoulders, and
that no man suffers that which he suffers. So let him lie (says God) without ease, until
he confess and repent and call for mercy.

W. Haller, *The Rise of Puritanism*, Columbia University Press/O.U.P., 1938, pp. 33-4

SOURCE 127 In Shakespeare's *Twelfth Night* two of the characters discuss Malvolio

Maria Marry, sir, sometimes he is a kind of puritan.

Sir Andrew O, if I thought that I'd beat him like a dog.

William Shakespeare, *Twelfth Night*, Act II scene iii

SOURCE 128 Puritans in state

A Puritan is he that speaks his mind
In Parliament; not looking once behind
To others' danger; nor just sideways leaning
To promised honour his direct true meaning
But for the laws and truth doth fairly stand . . .
His character abridged if you would have,
He's one that would a subject be, no slave.

'The Interpreter', attributed to Thomas Scot, in E. Arber, *An English Garner*, Vol. IV, London, 1895,
pp. 235-6

The growing threat

While the threat from the Catholics was effectively over in 1588 (though contemporaries did not realise this), the threat from the Puritans continued to grow. In 1588 the Queen had appointed Whitgift, Archbishop of Canterbury, so that he would enforce discipline in the Church of England and make the Puritans conform. In 1588 a series of pamphlets, published under the name of Martin Marprelate, was written, attacking the bishops. However, the attacks were so fierce and exaggerated that the pamphlets turned people against Puritanism rather than persuading them to follow it (sources 129, 130).

In the last decade of the reign the Puritans in religion and church policy were quieter, but they had not abandoned their aims. In Elizabeth's last Parliaments there was considerable opposition to her policies and demands for freedom of speech grew. This opposition was often described as Puritan, not just because it was against the government, but because Puritans, who were used to speaking freely in their religious discussions, were demanding similar rights in Parliament. While the Catholic threat was associated with a foreign interference in the government of England the Puritans challenged the Queen's powers to govern from within.

Elizabeth controlled such debates and divisions, within both the Church and Parliament, with difficulty in her later years. In the next century they were to break into open conflict.

RIGHT: John Stubbs having his hand cut off

SOURCE 129 Elizabeth takes action against the Puritans in 1583

From this time forward she [Elizabeth] began to be a little more incensed against the Puritans . . . And indeed within a few days after, John Stubbs of Lincolns-Inn, a fervent hot-headed Professor of religion, . . . the author of this book, William Page who dispersed the copies, and Singleton, the printer, were apprehended. Against whom sentence was given, that their right hands should be cut off . . . Hereupon Stubbs and Page had their right hands cut off with a cleaver, driven through the wrist by the force of a mallet, upon a scaffold in the market place at Westminster. The printer was pardoned. I remember (being there present) that when Stubbs, after his right hand was cut off, put off his hat with his left, and said with a loud voice, "God Save the Queen".

Camden, *History of the Princess Elizabeth*, MacCaffrey, p. 138

SOURCE 130 Archbishop Whitgift sets out to restore order in the Church of England

John Whitgift, being translated to Canterbury . . . the Queen gave in charge that he should take special care to restore the discipline of the Church of England, and the uniformity in the service of God established by authority of Parliament, which, through the connivance of the prelates, the obstinacy of the Puritans and the power of some noblemen was run out of square . . . as if there was no unity in the Church of England. To take away these inconveniences, and restore unity, he propounded these articles to be subscribed to by the ministers.

First, that the Queen has the chief and supreme power over all persons born within her dominions . . .

Secondly, that the Book of Common Prayer . . . might lawfully be used; and that they should use that, and no other form, either of prayer, or administration of the sacraments.

Camden, *History of the Princess Elizabeth*, MacCaffrey, pp. 162-3

ABOVE: John Whitgift, Archbishop of Canterbury

Elizabeth and Mary, Queen of Scots

Introduction

This case study falls into two main sections. Firstly it deals with Mary's arrival in England. It gives an account of the reasons why this should present a problem for Elizabeth. Secondly it provides evidence to help you answer the key question—What should be done with Mary, Queen of Scots?

Mary's arrival in England

In June 1567 Mary, Queen of Scots had been forced to abdicate from the Scottish throne and her son James VI had been proclaimed King. Mary was imprisoned in Lochleven Castle but on 2 May 1568 she escaped. She tried to regain the throne but failed and so she fled across the Solway Firth to England and landed at Workington on 16 May.

Her arrival in England as an uninvited royal guest created a problem for Queen Elizabeth and her Councillors. Why was this? Think about the following points.
1. Mary was Elizabeth's heir as Elizabeth, although she was thirty-five years old, was as yet unmarried and without children.
2. In 1558, Mary, Queen of Scots was married to Francis II, King of France. She was proclaimed Queen of England by the French when Mary Tudor died.

3. Mary was a Catholic and Catholics regarded her as the rightful Queen of England. They also wanted a Catholic or the English throne.

PAGE 87 RIGHT: The Arms of Mary, Queen of Scots

PAGE 87 FAR RIGHT: A letter written by Mary, Queen of Scots, aged 11, to her mother in Scotland

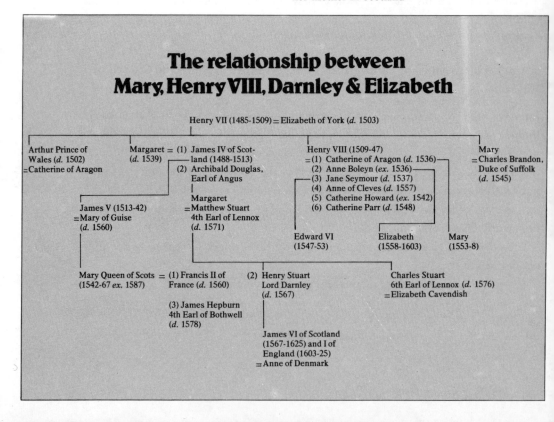

The relationship between Mary, Henry VIII, Darnley & Elizabeth

Henry VII (1485-1509) = Elizabeth of York (d. 1503)

Arthur Prince of Wales (d. 1502) = Catherine of Aragon

Margaret (d. 1539) = (1) James IV of Scotland (1488-1513)
(2) Archibald Douglas, Earl of Angus

Henry VIII (1509-47) = (1) Catherine of Aragon (d. 1536)
(2) Anne Boleyn (ex. 1536)
(3) Jane Seymour (d. 1537)
(4) Anne of Cleves (d. 1557)
(5) Catherine Howard (ex. 1542)
(6) Catherine Parr (d. 1548)

Mary = Charles Brandon, Duke of Suffolk (d. 1545)

James V (1513-42) = Mary of Guise (d. 1560)

Margaret = Matthew Stuart 4th Earl of Lennox (d. 1571)

Edward VI (1547-53)

Elizabeth (1558-1603)

Mary (1553-8)

Mary Queen of Scots (1542-67 ex. 1587) = (1) Francis II of France (d. 1560)
(2) Henry Stuart Lord Darnley (d. 1567)
(3) James Hepburn 4th Earl of Bothwell (d. 1578)

Charles Stuart 6th Earl of Lennox (d. 1576) = Elizabeth Cavendish

James VI of Scotland (1567-1625) and I of England (1603-25) = Anne of Denmark

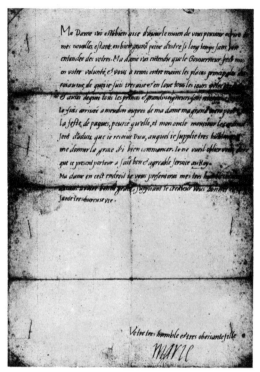

SOURCE 131 Killigrew Jones reports from the French court to Elizabeth, 29 November 1559

The French King departing from Blois on the 18th arrived at Châtellarault the 23rd inst., when he and the Queen made their entry. The latter came first, over whom carried by four townsmen a canopy of crimson damask with the arms of England, France and Scotland quartered thereupon. Over the King was a canopy of damask with the arms of France only.

The two gates of the town through which they passed were painted; on the right side were the arms of France with the King's name and on the left the arms of England, France and Scotland quartered with the Queen's name.

Joseph Stevenson (ed.), *Calendar of State Papers, Foreign*, Vol. II, HMSO, 1865, p. 145

SOURCE 132 A contemporary Catholic view of the succession

Finally the noblemen of this our Realm acknowledge and accept her for the very true and right Heir apparent of this Realm of England, being fully minded and always ready (when God shall so dispose) to receive and serve her as their undoubted Queen, Mistress and Sovereign.

John Leslie, Bishop of Ross, 'A Defence of the Honour of the Right High Mighty and Noble Princess Mary, Queen of Scotland', 1569, in J. Anderson (ed.), *Collections Relating to the History of Mary, Queen of Scotland*, Vol. I, Edinburgh, 1727-8, p. 81

What should be done with Mary, Queen of Scots?

Mary remained in England for the following nineteen years and various groups of people had differing ideas about what should be done with her.

Queen Elizabeth, her Councillors, her Members of Parliament, Catholics and Protestants both in England and in Europe held views about what should be done with Mary. Moreover, these views changed at different times during the period depending on the way people reacted to the various events.

In the pages which follow you will be able to study in both primary and secondary sources why views changed about what should be done with Mary, Queen of Scots during four different periods in time: 1568-70; 1570-2; 1580-4; 1586-7.

ABOVE: Mary, Queen of Scots wearing a hunting bonnet
RIGHT: Mary, Queen of Scots

1568-1570

Events

1. The English government held an inquiry into the reasons why Moray and the Scottish nobles had deposed Mary. This inquiry was held between 1568 and 1569 first at York and then in London. The main charges against Mary were her alleged part in the murder of her husband Darnley in February 1567 and her relationship with the Earl of Bothwell whom she had married in May 1567.

2. The inquiry was inconclusive. The Scottish lords were found not guilty of rebellion and Mary was found not guilty of the charges laid against her. However, she was not allowed to return to Scotland.

PAGE 89: Elizabeth I, standing on a map of England, c. 1592, by M. Gheeraerts the Younger

BELOW: Francis II of France, Mary, Queen of Scots' first husband

Instead she was kept at various places in England—at Carlisle, Castle Bolton in Wensleydale, Tutbury and then Sheffield for sixteen years with the Earl of Shrewsbury as her keeper.

3. In 1569 there was a plan to marry Mary to the Duke of Norfolk. It did not succeed.

4. In October 1569 some northern nobles including the Earls of Northumberland and Westmorland attempted a rebellion. Three of their aims were: to depose Elizabeth; to put Mary, Queen of Scots on the throne; and to restore Catholicism to England. The revolt was quelled by an army which Elizabeth sent north to deal with the rebels.

SOURCE 133 Elizabeth promises support to Mary, Queen of Scots, in a letter to Throckmorton, written on 11 August 1567

The more she considers these rigorous and unlawful proceedings of those lords against their sovereign lady, the more she is moved to consider how to relieve the Queen her sister . . . having cause to doubt that . . . they will increase their cruelty against her, whom they have it seems violently forced to leave her crown to an infant, to make her appear but a subject, and themselves, by gaining the government to become superior to her whom God and nature did create to be their head! . . . For as she is a princess if they continue to keep her in prison or touch her life or per-

son, she will not fail to revenge it to the uttermost.

Joseph Bain (ed.), *Calendar of Scottish Papers*, Vol. II, H. M. General Register House, 1900, p. 378

SOURCE 134 Elizabeth again promises support to Mary in her instructions to Leighton, 18 May 1568

The Queen commands him to express her joy to the Queen of Scots at her delivery from captivity . . . and to charge her subjects to submit to her, and if they would not, to let

them plainly understand, that . . . she will not want the assistance of that power which God has given her. And if she is content to stand to the Queen's order in comparing the controversies with her subjects, without soliciting aid from France, she shall receive all aid from the Queen either to persuade or to compel them . . . He shall declare to Mary the causes why his mistress deals in the matter i. She is next in her blood . . . ii. the meetest to do it, thinking her subjects will be advised by her . . .

Bain, *Scottish Papers*, Vol. II, p. 409

SOURCE 135 The plan to marry Mary to Norfolk, 1569

At this time a bruit [rumour] ran amongst men of better note, that the Duke of Norfolk should marry the Queen of Scots, which according to men's affections was upon different reasons desired, while the Papists hoped that hereby their religion would be advanced, and others that it would make for the good of the commonwealth. Certainly very many . . . thought it would make more for the settling of things, and the keeping the Queen of Scots within her bounds, "if she were joined in marriage to the Duke of Norfolk, the greatest and noblest man of all the nobility of England, a man in great favour with the people, and bred up in the Protestant religion, than if she were married to a foreign Prince, who might by her endanger both Kingdoms, and come to the inheritance of both . . ."

Amongst these consulters were the Earls of Arundel, Northumberland, Westmorland, Sussex, Pembroke, and Southampton, with many Barons, yea and Leicester also himself. All which notwithstanding were of opinion, that the matter was first to be imparted to the Queen, and left to her will and pleasure . . .

Soon after the rumour of this marriage came more clearly to Queen Elizabeth's ears, by means of the women of the Court, who do quickly smell out love-matters . . . the Queen took the Duke to her Board at Farnham, and pleasantly gave him warning "to beware upon what pillow he leaned his head".

The Queen then called the Duke unto her into a Gallery, and sharply chid him, that he had sought the Queen of Scots in marriage without acquainting her therewith, and commanded him upon his allegiance to give over that enterprise. The Duke willingly and readily promised so to do.

Camden, *History of the Princess Elizabeth*, pp. 126-30

RIGHT: Thomas Howard, Duke of Norfolk

SOURCE 136 Some support for the proposed marriage of Mary to Norfolk

Many of the English nobles, who themselves disliked the dominance of Cecil within the English Privy Council, and in addition felt that his foreign policy, so intensely hostile to Spain, was against England's best commercial interests, saw in the elevation of Norfolk as Mary's bridegroom a convenient way of dealing with Cecil's rising influence.

Antonia Fraser, *Mary Queen of Scots*, Panther, 1970, p. 492

SOURCE 137 The Privy Council's views about Mary, Queen of Scots

But whatsoever Queen Elizabeth's commiseration were towards her, the Council of England entered into serious deliberation what should be done with her. If she were detained in England, they feared lest she . . . might draw many daily to her part . . . Foreign ambassadors would further her counsels and designs; and the Scots then would not fail her, when they should see so rich a booty offered them . . . If she were sent over into France, they feared lest the Guises, her kinsmen, would prosecute her Title again, whereby she had laid claim to England . . .

Moreover the amity between England and Scotland, which was of special concernment, would be broken, and the ancient League between France and Scotland renewed, which would now be a matter of more dangerous consequence than in times past, when Burgundy was knit in a firm League with England . . .

If she should be sent back into Scotland, the fear was, lest those of the French party advanced to highest offices, the young Prince exposed to danger, religion in Scotland changed, the French and other foreigners let in, Ireland more greivously infested by the Hebridian Scots, and she herself brought into hazard of her life by her adversaries at home. Almost all of them therefore thought it best

RIGHT: Mary, Queen of Scots and her second husband Lord Darnley

BELOW: A section of a contemporary drawing, showing the scene at the time of Lord Darnley's murder

that she should be detained as taken by right of war, and not be delivered, till she gave satisfaction for unsurping the Title of England, and answered for the death of the Lord Darnley her husband, who was a native subject of England.

Camden, *History of the Princess Elizabeth*, pp. 110-11

SOURCE 138 Mary asks Elizabeth for better treatment

They [Mary's keepers] have forbid me to go out, and have rifled my trunks, entering my chamber with pistols and arms, not without putting me in bodily fear, and accusing my people, rifle them and place them under arrest; still I should have thought that in all this finding nothing which could affect or displease you, I should thereafter have experienced better treatment.

But seeing that such is the life I lead, with the prospect of its being worse, I presume to address to you this last request, containing the following:

. . . that you will be pleased, without longer putting me off for the sake of others to restore me to my own country and authority by your support, or to permit me, according to my former request, to retire to France to the Most Christian King my brother-in-law; or, at least, that during my imprisonment I may have liberty to communicate with the Bishop of Ross and other ministers necessary to settle my affairs; and that to these my affectionate requests you will send a reply, either by one of my people, or by letter from yourself.

From my prison at Tutbury, this 1st of October, Your very affectionate distressed sister and cousin.

Marie

A. Labanoff & A. Turnbull (eds.), *Letters of Mary Stuart*, London, 1845, pp. 173-4

SOURCE 139 The Earl of Northumberland was questioned about the Northern Rebellion

What was the intent and meaning of the rebellion?

Answer. Our first object in assembling was the reformation of religion and preservation of the person of the Queen of Scots, as next heir, failing issue of Her Majesty, which causes I believed were greatly favoured by most of the noblemen of the realm.

Green, *State Papers, Domestic*, Addenda, Vol. XXI, p. 407

BELOW: Tutbury Castle, from a drawing

SOURCE 140 Mary's attitude to the Northern Rebellion, according to a modern historian

The Northern rising in November, under the Catholic earls of Northumberland and Westmorland, did nothing to improve Queen Mary's lot. This rising, ill-prepared and ill-organised, was more in the nature of a separatist movement on the part of northern Catholics, than a revolt on behalf of Mary Queen of Scots. Queen Mary herself disapproved of it, not only on the grounds that she hated violence and wished to avoid the risk of slaughter of innocent people, but also on the very sensible grounds that she did not believe it would do her cause any good, since the movement was hardly ripe for such a demonstration.

Fraser, *Mary*, p. 497

SOURCE 141 Another historian's view of the situation

Mary's wisdom in fleeing to England in May 1568 has often been debated, but with her life in danger if she stayed in Scotland and unprepared for the longer voyage to France where her presence would not necessarily have been welcome, her choice of refuge was not an unreasonable one. Elizabeth's views on sovereignty and the duty of subjects were well known to Mary, and all things being equal, she might confidently have expected English assistance in regaining her throne. All things were not equal, however, for Mary was not only Elizabeth's heir, but had been proclaimed as queen of England. In such circumstances, Mary could not be allowed to go to France in which her claims to the English throne had first been pressed. On the other hand return to Scotland seemed equally impracticable as to repatriate Mary without military assistance would be to commit her to close captivity and probable execution, and to restore her by force would require the defeat of the pro-English party in that kingdom. If, however, Mary remained in England it seemed equally certain that her presence would provide a catalyst for all Elizabeth's

Mary Stuarts to be dealt with. One was the sister sovereign in exile, who merited honourable asylum and perhaps assistance to regain her throne. The other was the Catholic claimant to the English succession, if not to the English throne, the woman who would be under Elizabeth—only much more actively and dangerously—what Elizabeth had been under Mary Tudor, and Mary Tudor under Somerset and Northumberland, the magnet drawing together scattered elements of religious and political discontent.

How powerful a magnet Mary was her first eighteen months in England amply demonstrated. They saw the first of the reign's conspiracies and its only serious rebellion. Hitherto Elizabeth had kept England immune from such things . . .

S. T. Bindoff, *Tudor England*, Pelican, 1952, p. 207

disaffected subjects. Faced with such a dilemma, the English government took refuge in the idea of an enquiry at which Mary and Moray should both be represented.

I. B. Cowan, *The Enigma of Mary Stuart*, Sphere Books, 1972, p. 160

SOURCE 142 A modern historian's analysis of the problem

Mary's arrival set Elizabeth a problem which was only to be solved nineteen years later by her execution. There were really two

1570-1572

Events

1. The Pope excommunicated Elizabeth in 1570. This encouraged Catholic plots against Elizabeth.
2. In 1571 the Florentine, Ridolfi plotted to remove Queen Elizabeth and set Mary, Queen of Scots on the throne with the Duke of Norfolk as her consort. The plot failed, but both Mary and Norfolk were found to be involved.

ABOVE: Mary, Queen of Scots during her imprisonment, attributed to Pierre Oudry
LEFT: Mary, Queen of Scots, the Deuil Blanc portrait, c. 1559, by Francis Clouet

3. In January 1572 Norfolk was tried for high treason and in June he was executed.
4. On St Bartholomew's Day, 24 August 1572, thousands of French Protestants were killed. The massacre was begun by the Guises, Mary's French relatives.

SOURCE 143 Elizabeth expresses her fear of Mary in a sonnet 'The Doubt of Future Foes', which ends

The Daughter of Debate, that discord aye doth sow,
Shall reap no gain where former rule still peace hath taught to know.
No foreign banished wight shall anchor in this port;
Our realm brooks not seditious sects, let them elsewhere resort.
My rusty sword through rest shall first his edge employ,
To poll their tops that seek such change and gape for future joy.

L. Bradner, (ed.), *The Poems of Queen Elizabeth I*, Brown University Press, 1964, p. 4

SOURCE 144 Charges made by Parliament against Mary, Queen of Scots, in May 1572

i.   That she has wickedly and untruly challenged the present estate and possession of the crown of England and . . . usurped the style and arms of the same.

ii. That she has . . . sought by subtle means to withdraw the late Duke of Norfolk from his natural obedience and against Her Majesty's express prohibition to couple herself in marriage with the said Duke, to the intent that thereby she might . . . bring to effect Her Majesty's . . . destruction.

iii. That she has . . . stirred . . . the Earls of Northumberland and Westmorland . . . to rebel and levy open war against Her Majesty.

iv. That she has practised . . . to procure new rebellion to be raised within this realm. And for that intent she made choice of one Ridolphi, a merchant of Italy, who . . . solicited the said wicked enterprises to the Pope and other . . . confederates beyond the Seas.

v.   That the Pope has . . . put in bank 100,000 crowns to be employed upon any that would take upon him the setting up of Popish religion in this realm by helping her to the crown. And further that she was privy to that slanderous . . . Bull of Pope Pius against her Majesty.

. . . And although your Majesty of your most abundant goodness has hitherto, above the common limits and bonds of mercy, forborn to proceed against the said Mary according to her deserving . . . and considering also the most wicked . . . practices of her and her confederates . . . towards your Majesty do not cease but daily increase . . . we therefore, your true and obedient subjects, the Lords . . . and Commons in this present Parliament assembled, do most humbly beseech your Majesty . . . to punish and correct all the treasons and wicked attempts of the said Mary . . .

May it now therefore please your Majesty . . . that it may be enacted . . . in this present Parliament assembled, that the said Mary . . . shall not at any time have hold or claim . . . the title of the said crown of England . . . and that if the said Mary shall . . . make any claim . . . or stir any war or rebellion within the said realm of England and Ireland . . . the said Mary shall be deemed and taken a traitor to your Majesty.

Conyers Read (ed.), *The Bardon Papers, Documents Relating to the Imprisonment and Trial of Mary, Queen of Scots*, Camden Society, Third Series, Vol. 17, 1909, pp. 1–4, 113–23

ABOVE: The St. Bartholomew's Day Massacre, 24 August 1572

PAGE 94: The Ridolfi Plot, the illustration shows him as the link between the Pope and the rebels

SOURCE 145 A contemporary view of Elizabeth's refusal to follow the advice of Parliament

It is generally known unto the world that notwithstanding the manifest discovery of the said Queen's practice with the Duke of Norfolk, her procuring of the rebellion within the north parts of this realm and her practices with foreign princes abroad to have provoked them to have invaded this said realm . . . yet Her Majesty, being most earnestly pressed by the nobility and commons of this realm, in a Parliament held in the XIIIIth of her reign, to have proceeded against so dangerous a guest . . . did notwithstand (moved with a princely compassion towards the said unfortunate or rather unthankful Queen) forbear to satisfy the request of the said Lords to their great grief and infinite discontent.

Read, *Bardon Papers*, p.15

SOURCE 146 A modern historian's account of the difference in views between Elizabeth and her Parliaments

The English privy councillors proposed to bring her to trial for her sins, intending to make her pay as grim a penalty as Norfolk himself had done. Walsingham expressed their views in a letter which he wrote from Paris. "So long as that devilish woman lives", he wrote, "neither her Majesty must make account to continue in quiet possession of her crown, nor her faithful servants assure themselves of safety of their lives". Parliament was in substantial agreement. Both Houses joined to petition Elizabeth that the Queen of Scots, be "summarily dealt with", or failing that, that she be formally deprived of her rights of succession.

But Elizabeth opposed such extreme measures. She went so far as to send commissioners to Mary with instructions to demand her answers to the charges which had been made against her, but it soon became evident that she meant to go no further at least not in any direct line.

Read, *Bardon Papers*, Introduction, pp. xxvi-vii

SOURCE 147 Another modern historian's view

There is no doubt that had Elizabeth listened to her Parliament, Mary of Scotland would have died in 1572. Loyal Englishmen were convinced that she was an immoral and dangerous female and were determined to "cut off her head and make no more ado about her", but Elizabeth could not bring herself to execute a divinely ordained sovereign. To do so was impolitic (it set a dangerous precedent) and immoral (Mary was one of God's lieutenants on earth). So

Mary Stuart lived another fifteen years, surrounded by English spies but still possessed of a queen's household and always confident that some new plot might yet succeed.

L. Baldwin Smith, *The Elizabethan Epic*, Panther, 1969, p. 194

SOURCE 148 The view of Mary's latest biographer

Too little is known of Elizabeth's inner feelings for Mary, since the English queen had learnt in childhood to hide all inner feelings, those dangerous traitors, within the breast. That closeness which two queens and

near cousins should feel for each other, so often chanted by Mary, may have found more echoes in Elizabeth's heart than she ever admitted. In the meantime this merciful strain, this sneaking affection, could not fail to be noticed by Elizabeth's advisers; the point was taken that if ever the execution of Mary Stuart was to be secured, Elizabeth would have to be thoroughly convinced that her good sister had repaid her clemency with flagrant and harmful ingratitude.

Fraser, *Mary*, p. 509

ABOVE: Mary, Queen of Scots, a medal by Jacopo Primavera
ABOVE LEFT: Mary, Queen of Scots, c. 1578, a miniature by Nicholas Hilliard

1580-1584

Events

1. The Jesuit missions to England began in 1580.

2. In November 1583 the arrest of Francis Throckmorton revealed that Mary had been involved in negotiations with Spain.

3. In June 1584 William of Orange, the Protestant ruler of the Netherlands, was assassinated.

4. In November 1584 Parliament adopted the Bond of Association. This demanded the death penalty for all who plotted against Elizabeth and also for those who might benefit from such a plot.

5. Elizabeth negotiated for a treaty to free Mary in November 1584.

6. In January 1585 Mary was imprisoned more closely at Tutbury Castle under Sir Amias Paulet. Her mail was stopped for a year and then allowed to continue by Sir Francis Walsingham who set a trap to open any correspondence that Mary sent or received. As a result her agreement to Anthony Babington's plot to assassinate Elizabeth was discovered.

LEFT: The Spanish Ambassador being expelled from England after the discovery of the Throckmorton Plot 1583

RIGHT: The assassination of William of Orange, 1584

SOURCE 149 Offers made to Elizabeth by Mary, Queen of Scots, for her freedom, 21 April 1583

That she will accomplish the Treaty of Edinburgh, acknowledge Her Majesty and her lawful heirs most rightful successors to this crown of England.

That neither she nor her son . . . shall seek to . . . hurt her Majesty's person, government or estate . . .

That she will not deal with Pope, Jesuit, seminary priest or any others . . . in anything tending to the alteration of religion established by Her Majesty's authority, but will to the uttermost of her power resist them, and so make it known to the world . . . That because her remaining in Scotland or France cannot be without great suspicion to Her Majesty, she could be content to remain in some honourable sort in this realm as by Her Majesty and her Council might be advised . . .

That upon Her Majesty's pleasure to treat with her, she and her son will enter into any such perfect league as may be by Her Majesty and her Council thought most convenient for Her Majesty's safety during her life, and preservation of this realm afterwards from blood-shed, foreign invasion etc.

Read, *Bardon Papers*, pp. 17-19

RIGHT: Sir Christopher Hatton

SOURCE 150 Sir Christopher Hatton's summary of the arguments against freeing Mary written on 21 April 1583

She is the only instrument to work the overthrow of religion on this whole island . . .
Her title of succession shall be greatly advanced in credit by the opinion the world will conceive here of.
She may freely practise in any sort against the religion and this state without her own peril.
. . . it may prove dangerous to our party and the whole religion in Scotland. Besides it may be unacceptable to the King her son.

Read, *Bardon Papers*, pp. 19-20

SOURCE 151 Sir Christopher Hatton's arguments in favour of freeing Mary Stuart, written on 22 September 1584

First the Scottish Queen cannot endanger Her Majesty's state by her liberty so much as before time.

The present peril lieth much rather in the young King her son . . . He and she will repell the treasonable practise of Papists and Jesuits.

[The current hope of Catholic conspirators that Mary might be set up as a present competitor to Elizabeth for the English throne] fully extinguished.

Peril of violence towards the Queen's person happily avoided.
All outward attempts of foreign princes stayed.
A league defensive with Scotland concluded.

Read, *Bardon Papers*, pp. 23-4

SOURCE 152 A contemporary historian describes Mary's reaction to the Bond of Association

The Queen of Scots, who easily perceived that her destruction was aimed at by this Association, being weary of her long misery, and fearing harder measure, propounded these things following to the Queen and Council by Naw her Secretary.

That if her Liberty might be granted her, and she might be assured of Queen Elizabeth's sincere affection and love towards her, she would enter into a closer amity with the Queen, officiously love and observe her above all other Princes in Christendom, forget all by-past displeasures, acknowledge her to be the true and rightful Queen of England, forbear to pretend or lay claim to the Crown of England, during her life attempt nothing against her directly or indirectly, flatly renounce the Title and Arms of England, which she had usurped by the command of King Francis her husband, as likewise the Pope's Bull for her Deposing, yea and enter also into the aforesaid Association for the Queen's Security, and into a League defensive, (so far as might stand with the ancient League betwixt France and Scotland). Provided that nothing should be done during the Queen's life, or after her death, which might prejudice her, her son, and their heirs, in the succession, before such time as they were heard in an Assembly of the Estates of England. That for confirmation hereof, she herself would stay a while in England as an hostage.

She prayed that a speedy answer might be returned hereunto ... And lastly, she besought that she might be kept in freer custody, that thereby the Queen's love towards her might be more plainly discerned.

These things, as savouring of much respect and honour, Q. Elizabeth seemed to take great pleasure and contentment in; and it was believed she was then really purposed to set her at liberty; though there wanted not some in England who, by laying new fears before her, deterred her from it. But the business, which was as good as concluded, was quite hindered and dashed by the Scots of the contrary faction, who cried out, "That there was no hope of Queen Elizabeth's safety, if she were set at liberty; That both Kingdoms were undone, if she were admitted to be partner with her son in the Kingdom; that the true religion in Britain was ruined, if the exercise of the Romish religion were allowed her, though it were but within the court-walls."

Camden, *History of the Princess Elizabeth*, pp. 300-1

SOURCE 153 A modern historian's account of the negotiations for a treaty in 1584

To renew the negotiations for the treaty with Mary in the temper of the year 1584 was an amazing thing for Elizabeth to do. Yet renewed they were, only to drag along drearily owing to the confusion of Anglo-Scottish relations. Despair, anger, and a reckless foolishness seized Mary. Time and again, when talking to English officials, she called God to witness and vowed the most solemn oaths that she knew of no conspiracy against Elizabeth nor would consent to any; but her soul was no sooner forsworn, than she was writing to the conspirators to

ABOVE: Elizabeth I, c. 1575

launch the invasion without thought of the peril to her. Told of the Bond of Association, she offered to subscribe it: nevertheless, two days later she bade her friends go forward with the "Enterprise" whatever became of her, whether Elizabeth made a treaty with her or not. When this letter was written, early in November, the treaty was actually under way again, and Mary's secretary was setting out for the Court, there to join with an ambassador from James.

Had James really desired and been able to associate his mother in the crown of Scotland, at the same time making an alliance with Elizabeth, nothing seems clearer than that the treaty would now have been concluded, English statesmen, drawing up the pros and cons, found the arguments for it outweigh those against. Elizabeth herself broke a vow that she had made fourteen years before, and wrote to Mary in her own hand.

Mary believed in her son. She also trusted his ambassador, who belonged to her party and was deep in her perilous secrets. But perfidy was no monopoly of hers. Son and ambassador were both playing her false. James wanted an alliance with Elizabeth, but did not want to share his crown; nor, indeed, did he want his mother set free. That was the shattering truth, and it could no longer be hidden.

J. E. Neale, *Queen Elizabeth I*, Pelican, 1971, p. 269

SOURCE 154 Evidence is found to convict Mary of treason

The . . . letter was in Walsingham's hands by Tuesday 19 July. . . . On 29 July Babington himself received the . . . letter and deciphered it the next day with the help of Tichborne. On 3rd August he wrote back to the Scottish queen acknowledging the fatal letter. By this date, however, as Mary's hopes of release began to rise, one of Walsingham's agents, William Wade, had already secretly visited Chartley to work out with Paulet the best manner of securing her arrest . . . Babington fled north through London to the leafy lanes of St. John's Wood; here he lay in safety for sometime, until on 14th August he too was seized, and brought in hideous triumph to the Tower.

Fraser, *Mary*, p. 580

RIGHT: The trial of Mary, Queen of Scots at Fotheringay Castle in 1586, a contemporary drawing

PAGE 101: The embroidery said to have been worked by Mary, Queen of Scots and the Countess of Shrewsbury during Mary's captivity

1586-1587

Events
1. After the execution of Babington, Mary was tried at Fotheringay in October 1586. She was found guilty of treason.
2. On 1 February 1587 Elizabeth signed the death warrant for Mary.
3. On 8 February 1587 Mary was executed and Elizabeth claimed that although she had signed the death warrant she had not intended it to be sent.

SOURCE 155 Sentence of death passed on Mary, Queen of Scots

On the said 25th day of October all the Commissioners met, except the Earls of Shrewsbury and Warwick, which were both of them sick at that time. And after Nawe and Curle had upon Oath, viva voce, voluntarily, without hope of reward, avowed, affirmed and justified all and every the letters and copies of letters before produced to be true and real, sentence was pronounced against the Queen of Scots, and confirmed by the Seals and Subscriptions of the Commissioners, and recorded in these words. "By their unanimous Assents and Consents they do pronounce and deliver this their Sentence and Judgment, at the Day and Place last above recited, and say, that since the Conclusion of the aforesaid Session of Parliament divers Matters have been compassed and imagined within this Realm of England by Anthony Babington and others, in English, with the privity of the said Mary, pretending a Title to the Crown of this Realm of England, tending to the Hurt, Death and Destruction of the Royal Person of our said Lady the Queen . . . contrary to the Form of the Statute in the Commission aforesaid specified."

Camden, *History of the Princess Elizabeth*, pp. 361-2

SOURCE 156 Arguments urging the execution of Mary Stuart written during 1586-7 in a paper found in Sir Christopher Hatton's possession

Her Majesty in not executing justice upon the Scottish Queen shall foster and nourish that only hope which the Catholics have to re-establish their religion within this realm.

The Scottish Queen's life cannot stand with Her Majesty's safety and quiet estate of this realm, being as she is the only ground of all practises and attempts both at home and abroad.

Mercy and Pity . . . is nothing else but cruel kindness; but in the Scottish Queen experience teaches that the more favour she receives the more mischief she attempts.

Where public safety . . . enforces a speedy execution (as in this case it does) there ought no respect either of kindred, affection, honour or any other whatsoever to enforce the contrary. What dishonour . . . were it, in sparing the life of so grievous an offender, to hazard the lives of so many thousands of true subjects, being left to the . . . revenge of so malicious a woman. By taking away the Scottish Queen's life Her Majesty shall quench the malice of foreign Princes who, notwithstanding they will not be quiet during her life, will never trouble themselves to revenge her death.

If Her Majesty shall omit this occasion to take away so dangerous a person, when law and justice condemneth her, there may hereafter more dangerous practices be attempted when law and justice cannot take hold of her.

Read, *Bardon Papers*, Vol. 18, pp. 93-5

SOURCE 157 Another point of view; some contemporaries thought that the sentence on Mary was too harsh

Some indifferent Censurers there were who thought she was too sharply dealt with all, and had hard measure, in regard she was a free and absolute Princess, and had no superiour but God alone; they said, she was Queen Elizabeth's very near Kinswoman, who had made her a large Promise, on the Word of a Prince, of all Courtesie and kind Hospitality, as soon as she was arrived in England, being thrown out of her Kingdom by her rebels; and yet on the contrary had kept her still in prison, and violated the sacred rights of hospitality; that she could not be otherways reputed than as a prisoner taken in war; and it was always lawful for such as were taken prisoners in war, to use what means they could to work their own safety and liberty; that she could not commit treason, because she was no subject, and Princes of equal Degree have no power or Sovereignty one over another. Moreover, that it was a thing never heard of, that a Prince should be subjected to the Stroke of an Executioner.

Camden, *History of the Princess Elizabeth*, p. 370

RIGHT: Mary, Queen of Scots in Captivity

PAGE 103 LEFT: Mary, Queen of Scots, a memorial portrait

PAGE 103 RIGHT: The Earl of Shrewsbury

SOURCE 158 A conflicting contemporary viewpoint; some thought that Mary could rightfully be executed

Others there were who took her not to be a free and absolute Queen, but a Titular Queen only, because she had resigned her Kingdom, and when she first came into England had put herself under the protection of the Queen of England; after which, as by carrying herself well she enjoyed the benefit of the Laws, so by misdemeanor she was subject to the equity and justice thereof . . .

They reputed her also to be Subject because two absolute Princes with Regal Authority cannot be in the same Kingdom at one time. That it was a received opinion of the learned in the laws, a King out of his own Dominions (except it be upon a warlike Expedition) is but a private person, and therefore can neither confer honours, nor exercise any royalty. Moreover, that she by her misdemeanours had lost her absolute and just power and sovereignty.

Camden, *History of the Princess Elizabeth*, p. 371

SOURCE 159 Petition of Parliament against Mary, presented to Elizabeth 12 November 1586

And to move Her Majesty thereunto, the said speaker of the House of Commons did use many excellent and solid reasons which were all found in a certain Memorial written with his own hand, being as followeth.

Unless execution of this just sentence be done

1. Your Majesty's Person cannot any while be safe.

2. The Religion cannot long continue amongst us.

3. The most flourishing present state of this realm must shortly receive a woeful fall.

4. And consequently in sparing her your Majesty shall not only give courage and tardiness to the enemies of God, of your Majesty's self, and of your Kingdom; but shall discomfort and daunt with despair the hearts of your loving people and so deservedly provoke the heavy hand and wrath of God.

D'Ewes, *Journal of the Parliaments of Elizabeth*, p. 400

SOURCE 160 Queen Elizabeth told Parliament of her difficulty in deciding what to do with Mary

But I must tell you one thing, that by this last Act of Parliament you have reduced me to such Straits and Perplexities, that I must

resolve upon the punishment of her who is a Princess so nearly allied to me in blood, and whose practices against me have so deeply affected me with grief and sorrow, that I have willingly chosen to absent myself from this Parliament, lest I should increase my trouble by hearing the matter mentioned . . .

The Association you entered into for my safety I have not forgotten, a thing I never so much as thought of, till a great number of hands and seals to it were shewed me. This hath laid a perpetual tie and obligation upon me to bear you a singular goodwill and love, who have no greater comfort than in your

and the Commonwealth's respect and affection towards me . . . I hope you do not look for any present resolution from me: for my manner is, in matters of less moment than this, to deliberate long upon that which is but once to be resolved. In the mean time I beseech Almighty God so to illuminate and direct my heart, that I may see clearly what may be best for the good of his Church, the prosperity of the Commonwealth, and your safety. And that delay may not breed danger we will signifie our resolution to you with all conveniency . . .

Camden, *History of the Princess Elizabeth*, pp. 364-5

SOURCE 161 Elizabeth signs the death warrant for Mary, Queen of Scots

In the midst of these doubtful and perplexed thoughts, which so troubled and staggered the Queen's mind, that she gave herself wholly over to solitariness, sate many times melancholick and mute, and frequently sighing muttered this to herself. Aut fer, aut feri, that is, Either bear with her, or smite her, and, out of I know not what emblem, Ne feriare, feri, that is, Strike, lest thou be stricken, she delivered a writing to Davison, one of the Secretaries signed with her own hand, commanding a Warrant under the Great Seal of England to be drawn up for the Execution, which should lie in readiness if any danger chanced to break forth in that time of jealousie and fear; and, commanded him to acquaint no man therewith. But the next day, while fear seemed to be afraid of her own counsels and designs, her mind changed, and she commanded Davison by William Killegrew that the Warrant should not be drawn. Davison came presently to the Queen, and told her that it was drawn and under Seal already. She was somewhat moved at it, and blamed him for making such haste. He notwithstanding acquainted the Council both with the Warrant and the whole matter easily persuaded them, who were apt to believe what they desired, that the Queen had commanded it should be executed. Hereupon without any delay Beale (who in respect of Religion was of all others the Queen of Scots most bitter adversary) was sent down, with one or two executioners, and a Warrant, wherein authority was given to the Earls of Shrewsbury, Kent, Derby, Cumberland, and others, to see her executed according to the Law; and this without any knowledge of the Queen at all. And though she at that very time told Davison that she would take another course with the Queen of Scots, yet did not he for all that call Beale back.

Camden, *History of the Princess Elizabeth*, p. 382

SOURCE 162 Elizabeth claims she is innocent of Mary's death in letters to James VI of Scotland, Mary, Queen of Scots' son

God, the searcher of all hearts, ever so have misericorde of my soul, as my innocency in that matter deserveth, and no otherwise; which invocation were too dangerous for a guilty conscience.

J. Bruce (ed.), *Letters of Queen Elizabeth and King James VI of Scotland*, Camden Society, 1909, pp. 43–4

SOURCE 163 Another letter from Elizabeth to James VI of Scotland

My dearest Brother, I would to God thou knewest (but not that thou feltest) the incomparable grief my mind is perplexed with upon this lamentable accident, which is happened contrary to my meaning and intention, which, since my pen trembleth to mention it, you shall fully understand by this my kinsman. I request you, that as God and many others can witness my innocency in this matter, so you will also believe, that if I commandeth it, I would never deny it, I am not so faint-hearted, that for terrour I should fear to doe the thing which is just; or to own it when it is once done: no, I am not so base not ignobly minded. But as it is no Princely part, with feigned words to conceal and disguise the real making of the heart; so will I never dissemble my actions, but make them appear in their true and proper colours. Persuade yourself this for truth, that as I know this is happened deservedly on her part, so if I had intended it, I would not have laid it upon others; but I will never charge myself with that which I had not so much as thought of.

Camden, *History of the Princess Elizabeth*, p. 388

PAGE 104 LEFT: Bess of Hardwick, the Countess of Shrewsbury
PAGE 104 RIGHT: The execution of Mary, Queen of Scots, a contemporary drawing

SOURCE 164 Parliament approves the execution of Mary, Queen of Scots, February 1587

The same time Mr. Cromwell moved the House for that at their petition Her Majesty had done justice upon the Scottish Queen to the greater safeguard of Her Majesty's person and the whole realm he thought it fit that Her Majesty might receive from them their humble thanks; which motion was well liked, but at this time it proceedeth no further.

D'Ewes, *Journal of the Parliaments of Elizabeth*, p. 407

SOURCE 165 A modern historian's summary

On 8 February 1587 Mary Queen of Scots was executed at Fotheringay Castle. During her nineteen years in England Mary had repeatedly committed what in any of Elizabeth's subjects would have been high treason. She had been implicated in practically every plot against Elizabeth, and it was abundantly clear that given the opportunity she would have stopped at nothing which promised her the liberty that she had lost or the crown that she still hoped to gain. Surely she deserved the death which she had done so much to contrive for another. So thought every one of Elizabeth's parliaments, so thought all her ministers and councillors. And it was her Secretary, Walsingham, who early in 1586 set the trap which proved Mary's connivance at yet another plot; it was the parliament of 1586 which extorted from Elizabeth the death sentence against her; and it was the privy council which in the end shouldered the responsibility of sending it off to Fotheringay. Elizabeth's long refusal to take the step which almost any of her subjects, in her place, would have taken long before was a mixture of sentiment and reason not unlike that which had earlier determined her, also in defiance of the nation's earnest wish, to refuse to marry. Her womanly tenderness fought against taking the life of a woman, her regal loyalty against taking the life of one who had been a queen. But may not her reason also have told her, as, indeed, experience had proved, that if a pretender was a magnet to disaffection, a pretender in captivity was a key to its exposure? Elizabeth never acted solely out of sentiment, and if she had earlier judged Mary's death a necessity, she would not have shrunk from its cruelty. When, at last, she yielded—although even then she left the final responsibility to others—the argument for Mary's death was overwhelmingly strong . . . Mary living would be infinitely more dangerous than Mary dead. Justice had long demanded that Mary should die, but it was expediency not justice, that sent her to her death in 1587.

Bindoff, *Tudor England*, pp. 245-6

REGINAM·SERENISS·MA REGVM FILIAM,
VXOREM ET MATREM, ASTANTIBVS
COMMISSARIIS ET MINISTRIS R·
ELIZABETHÆ CARIFEX SECVRI
PERCVTIT ATQ·VNO ET ALTERO
ICTV TRVCVLENTER SAVCIATÆ
TERTIO EI CAPVT ABSCINDIT,

SOURCE 166 Another modern historian's summary

That there were men plotting to free Mary and kill Elizabeth was certain, but Walsingham wanted proof of Mary's complicity since he was convinced that the danger could only end if the rival queen were dead. To that purpose he so arranged matters that ever since men have been found to say that he invented the plot for which Mary was executed. The truth is that Mary was guilty, but Walsingham tricked her into giving herself away. In December 1585 he had her transferred to Chartley Manor, and there, with the assistance of Paulet and a renegade catholic, persuaded her that she had found a safe way to communicate with France.

In reality, every letter to and fro passed through the secretary's hands. By the middle of 1586 the new conspiracy was taking shape in the mind of Anthony Babington, a young man of more devotion than sense, and by July Mary was in Walsingham's toils. Babington wrote her a full account of the plot—which involved the assassination of Elizabeth—and asked her approval. There is both drama and disgust in the scene that followed, with Walsingham and his agents tensed in their wait for Mary's answer. It was delayed and all seemed lost; at last it came, and the queen of Scots was seen to have given her approval to everything. It was the end. By September the conspirators were executed—to the joy of the populace—and in October a special commission tried Mary and found her guilty. Guilty she was, but Elizabeth felt no more inclined now than earlier to exact the penalty. A fellow queen whose links with France made her execution a serious international matter—all Elizabeth's humane and political instincts rose up against the action. But the nation and the council were determined. Once more parliament, pressing for Mary's death, was put off with an "answer answerless", but on 1 February 1587 Elizabeth yielded and signed the warrant. She would not let it go; she tried to get Paulet to act in secret which that narrow but upright man refused angrily; then the council, acting without her knowledge, despatched the warrant. On the 7th Mary mounted the scaffold in Fotheringay Castle and welcomed martyrdom, expiating her sins and also creating a legend and a continued attachment which no other death could have produced.

Elizabeth was distraught. Her rage over-topped all previous experiences of that awesome natural phenomenon. All the council were in disgrace: there was talk of prosecuting them for murder. William Davison, the second secretary of state who had let the warrant out of his keeping, was fined heavily and committed to the Tower. But the wrath passed, Burghley, Leicester and the rest returned to favour. Davison, the scapegoat was released, and though he relinquished his appointment he continued to draw his fee.

G. R. Elton, *England Under the Tudors*, Methuen, 1965, pp. 368-70

PAGE 106: The execution of Mary, Queen of Scots, details from the memorial portrait

BELOW: The effigy of Mary, Queen of Scots on her tomb in Westminster Abbey

RIGHT: George Gascoigne, poet and
dramatist, presents one of his
works to Elizabeth I, c. 1579

5

The theatre of Shakespeare

During Elizabeth's reign the English theatre burst into life. In one generation play acting attained the greatest heights of poetry and drama.

Plays had been one of the most popular forms of entertainment through the Middle Ages. They were usually performed by wandering groups of actors, who went from village to village, often performing in the inn yard. Other groups of entertainers—minstrels, jugglers and acrobats—toured towns and villages too, but they were classed with the rogues and vagabonds who also roamed the countryside and were liable to be imprisoned (source 167).

From such a motley crowd Shakespeare and his contemporary playwrights trained their actors. Theatre-going became fashionable and popular, and Elizabeth even invited the companies to perform for her at Court (sources 168, 169).

Companies of actors also performed at great country houses. These private performances continued even after the public theatres had opened in the second half of Elizabeth's reign. When public performances were held in the afternoon, the private ones were held in the evening. Private performances helped to keep theatre alive during the later years of the

LEFT: A conjuror

reign, when Puritans in London condemned public performances of plays.
When London theatres closed because of
the plague performances were continued at
various country houses.

SOURCE 167 Actors were thought of as rogues and vagabonds

Among rogues and idle persons, finally, we find to be comprised all proctors that go up
and down with counterfeit licences, cozeners and such as gad about the country using
unlawful games, practisers of physiognomy and palmistry, tellers of fortunes, fencers,
players, minstrels, jugglers, pedlers, tinkers . . .

Harrison, *Description of England*, p. 186

SOURCE 168 Elizabeth approved of the theatre and went to performances

Our late Queen Elizabeth of Blessed memory . . . how well she approved of these
recreations, being as she termed them "harmless spenders of time" . . . Neither did she
hold it any derogation to that royal and princely majesty, which she then in her regal
person presented, to give some countenance to their endeavours, whereby they might
be the better encouraged in their action.

Richard Brathwait, *The English Gentleman*, London, 1641, p. 106

SOURCE 169 Sometimes Elizabeth invited a company of actors to the Court to perform

To the Lord Chamberlain's players upon the Council's Warrant dated at Whitehall,
25th February 1579, in consideration of a play by them presented before Her Majesty on
St. Stephen's Day last past, £6. 13s. 4d. and more in reward by Her Majesty, 66s. 8d. in
all £10.

D. Cook & F. P. Wilson (eds.), 'Dramatic Records in the Accounts of the Treasurer of the Chamber,
1558-1642', in *Collections*, Vol. VI, The Malone Society, 1961-62, p. 17

The theatres

The first permanent theatre was built in London in 1576 and was called simply the Theatre. Three other theatres, the Curtain, the Rose and the Swan had all been built before the best known of all, the Globe, was opened on Bankside in 1599. This is the theatre most closely associated with Shakespeare (sources 170, 171).

The design of the new theatres is often thought to have shown the influence of the inn yard and its stage, where the companies used to act. The design of the new buildings may well have been influenced by those of ancient Greece and Rome.

The time when Shakespeare was writing was the age of the Renaissance. This was a period of renewed interest in the ideas and culture of the ancient Greek and Roman societies. Travellers returned to England with exciting stories of the places they had visited and of the artists and poets who were working in Italy and other parts of Europe. They also came back with memories of the beautiful buildings they had seen and used many classical designs in the new houses that they built for themselves. It is quite possible that they also used their knowledge of Greek and Roman theatre design when new theatres were built in England. The men who built the London theatres may also have been influenced by John Dee, one of the leading mathematicians of the day. From his studies in Europe he was convinced that the architecture and the design of buildings should be based on mathematical principles. In particular the concept of proportion was very important.

ABOVE: Edward Alleyn

SOURCE 170 **A description of the structure of the Fortune Theatre built in 1600 (they dated their year from Ladyday 25th March, not 1 January)**

THIS INDENTURE made the eighth day of January, 1599 [1600] and in the two and fortieth year of the reign of our sovereign Lady Elizabeth . . . Between Philip Henslowe and Edward Alleyn of the parish of Saint Saviour's in Southwark . . . on the one part, And Peter Street, citizen and carpenter of London on the other part . . .

The frame of the said house to be set square, and to contain fourscore foot of lawful assize every way square without and fifty five foot of like assize square every way within, with a good, sure, and strong foundation of piles, brick, lime and sand, both without and within, to be wrought one foot of assize at the least above the ground.

And the said frame to contain three stories in height . . . All which stories shall contain . . . four convenient divisions for gentlemen's rooms, and other sufficient and convenient divisions for twopenny rooms, with necessary seats to be placed and set as well in these rooms as throughout all the rest of the galleries of the said house . . . as are made and contrived in and to the late erected playhouse on the Bank . . . called the Globe.

With a Stage and Tiring-house to be made . . . with a shadow or cover over the said stage . . . Which stage shall contain in length forty and three foot of lawful assize, and in breadth to extend to the middle of the yard of the said house.

W. W. Greg (ed.), *Henslowe's Diary*, A. H. Bullen, 1907, pp. 4-5

SOURCE 171 The London theatres are described by De Witt in about 1596

There are in London four theatres of noteworthy beauty, which bear diverse names according to their diverse signs. In them a different action is daily presented to the people. The two finest of these are situated to the southward beyond the Thames, named, from the signs they display, the Rose and the Swan. The two others are outside the city towards the north . . . There is also a fifth, of dissimilar structure, devoted to beast-baiting, wherein many bears, bulls, and dogs of stupendous size are kept in separate dens and cages, which being pitted against each other, afford men a most delightful spectacle. Of all the theatres, however, the largest and most distinguished is that whereof the sign is a swan . . . since it has space for three thousand persons, and is built of a concrete of flint stones . . . and supported by wooden columns, painted in such excellent imitations of marble that it might deceive even the most prying . . . Its form seems to approach that of a Roman structure.

Cyril Walter Hodges, *The Globe Restored: a Study of the Elizabethan Theatre*, Ernest Benn, 1953, pp. 94-5

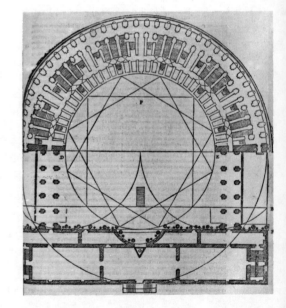

RIGHT: Palladio's plan of a Roman theatre

The design of the theatres

It is very difficult to imagine just what an Elizabethan theatre looked like because we have very few contemporary pictures or descriptions. The main source of information is a drawing of the Swan. There was a central space open to the sky, known as the 'yard'. The stage projected into the yard and at the back of it was a roofed area. The underside of this cover was painted with representations of the heavens. Behind the open stage was the 'tiring house', which the actors used as a dressing room. Round the open central area were three tiers of roofed seats.

The open space provided the daylight necessary to see the play. Plays were performed in the afternoon, unless the weather was bad. A flag flew from the roof of the theatre to show people that a play would definitely be performed that day.

The stage

The fact that the stage protruded into open space where most of the audience stood meant that actors and audience were very close to each other. The Elizabethan stage did present certain problems to the playwright. The auditorium was open to the sky, and there was no curtain across

ABOVE: The Fortune theatre
LEFT: An Elizabethan stage

To the Reader.

This *Figure*, that thou here feeft put,
It was for gentle *Shakespeare* cut;
Wherein the *Graver* had a ftrife
With *Nature*, to out-doe the *Life*:
O, could he but have drawn his *Wit*
As well in *Braffe*, as he has hit
His *Face*; the *Print* would then furpaffe
All, that was ever writ in *Braffe*.
But fince he cannot, *Reader*, look
Not on his *Picture*, but his *Book*.

ABOVE: William Shakespeare, the Droeshout portrait

the stage as there is in most theatres today. Audiences did not sit in respectful silence, and writers had to find a way of seizing people's attention at the beginning of the play without the benefit of lowering lights and a slowly drawn back curtain. The time of day or night had to be indicated by what the actors said, rather than by elaborate lighting effects.

As there was no curtain to signal the end of one scene and the beginning of the next, the action was continuous, as in a modern film. This sometimes created problems. In Shakespeare's *Macbeth*, for example, after the murder of Duncan, Macbeth and Lady Macbeth are startled to hear a knock at the door of the castle. If the new arrivals catch them dressed, as

they are, in their day clothes, they will suspect them of the murder. They need time, therefore, in which to go off stage to change into their night clothes, so that they can pretend they were in bed when the murder was committed. To provide the necessary delay, Shakespeare makes the Porter, who has to open the door, drunk (source 172). Another way of giving the actors time to change was by introducing several plots, with different groups of actors, within one play. As there was little scenery and no time to change it as the action of the play moved forward the words of the play had to tell the audience where they should imagine the scene taking place (sources 173-175).

SOURCE 172 Shakespeare has to give Macbeth and Lady Macbeth time to get off the stage and change their clothes

Lady Macbeth   [*Knocking within*]
. . . I hear a knocking.
At the south entry: retire we to our chamber;
A little water clears us of this deed:
How is it then! Your constancy
Hath left you unattended [*Knocking within*]
Hark! more knocking.
Get on your night-gown, lest occasion call us,
And show us to be watchers. Be not lost
So poorly in your thoughts.
Macbeth. To know my deed, 'twere best not know myself.   [*Knocking within*]
Wake Duncan with thy knocking: I would thou couldst!   [*Exeunt*

SCENE III,

The same Knocking within.

Enter a Porter.

Porter Here's a knocking, indeed! If a man were porter of hell-gate, he should have old [Nick] turning the key. [*Knocking within*] Knock, knock, knock! Who's there, i' the name of Beelzebub? . . .

William Shakespeare, *Macbeth*, Act II, scene ii, iii

SOURCE 173 The Chorus in the Prologue to *Henry V* describes Shakespeare's theatre, the Globe

. . . But pardon, gentles all,
The flat unraised spirits that have dared
On this unworthy scaffold to bring forth
So great an object; can this cockpit hold
The vasty fields of France? or may we cram
Within this wooden O the very casques
That did affright the air at Agincourt?

William Shakespeare, *Henry V*, Prologue

SOURCE 174 In *Hamlet* the opening words of the play had to tell the audience what time it was

Enter Bernardo, and Francisco, two Sentinels

Ber. Who's there?

Fran. Nay, answer me: stand and unfold yourself.

Ber. Long Live the King!

Fran. Bernardo?

Ber. He.

Fran. You come most carefully upon your hour.

Ber. 'Tis now struck twelve; get thee to bed, Francisco.

William Shakespeare, *Hamlet*, Act I, scene i

ABOVE: A contemporary drawing of the Swan theatre

Thunder and lightning. Enter three Witches

Shakespeare, *Macbeth*, Act I, scene i

BELOW: A circus performance in the theatre

28   LOVE'S LABOUR'S LOST.

Arm. I will hereupon confefs, I am in love: and, as it is bafe for a foldier to love, fo am I in love with a bafe wench. If drawing my fword againft the humour of affeċtion would deliver me from the reprobate thought of it, I would take defire prifoner, and ranfom him to any French courtier for a new devifed courtefy. I think fcorn to figh; methinks, I fhould out-fwear Cupid. Comfort me, boy: What great men have been in love?

Moth. Hercules, mafter.

Arm. Moft fweet Hercules!—More authority,

STEEVENS.

Opposition to the theatre

Theatres were used for other forms of entertainment as well as plays, in which case the stage was not used. Sometimes the ground area was used for baiting bears and other animals (sources 176, 177). This part of a modern theatre is still called the 'pit'. At other times performances like present day circuses were put on. No doubt these entertainments made the Puritans associate plays with the theatre of ancient Rome, where people, particularly Christians, as well as animals were killed. No wonder they objected to theatre so strongly (sources 178-180).

SOURCE 176 **Animal-baiting and circus entertainment in the theatre was described by a European visitor in 1585**

We walked across the bridge to Southwark. Here there is a round building with three corridors built one above the other. Here there were close upon one hundred great English dogs, each of which had a special kennel made of boards. Here in a building, three bears, each larger than the other, were baited one after another by some dogs. Then a horse was brought in, and it too was baited. Then an ox was led in. This ox suffered a game resistance. Then out of a mechanical contrivance there came forth various males and females who danced, sang and spoke. Lastly a man came out and scattered bread among the crowd, who scrambled for it.

Victor von Klarwill, *Queen Elizabeth and Some Foreigners*, T. H. Nash (trans.), Bodley Head, 1928, p. 315

SOURCE 177 **A German visitor describes English theatres and bear gardens**

Without the city are some theatres, where English actors represent almost every day tragedies and comedies to very numerous audiences; these are concluded with excellent music, variety of dances, and the excessive applause of those that are present.

There is still another place, built in the form of a theatre, which serves for the baiting of bulls and bears; they are fastened behind, and then worried by great English bulldogs but not without great risk to the dogs, from the horns of the one and the teeth of the other; and it sometimes happens that they are killed upon the spot; fresh ones are immediately supplied in the place of those that are wounded or tired. To this entertainment there often follows that of whipping a blinded bear, which is performed by five or six men, standing circularly with whips, which they exercise upon him without any mercy, as he cannot escape from them because of his chain; he defends himself with all his force and skill, vigorously throwing down all who come within his reach and are not active enough to get out of it, and tearing the whips out of their hands and breaking them. At these spectacles and everywhere else, the English are constantly smoking tobacco . . . In these theatres, fruits, such as apples, pears and nuts, according to the season, are carried about to be sold, as well as ale and wine.

Hentzner, *Travels in England*, pp. 41-3

ABOVE: A reconstruction of the stage at the Globe theatre

SOURCE 178 **Puritan opposition to the theatre**

Look upon the common plays in London, and see the multitude that flocketh to them and followeth them. Behold the sumptuous theatre houses, a continual monument of London's prodigality and folly. But I understand they are now forbidden because of the plague. I like the policy well if it hold still, for a disease is but lodged or patched up that is not cured in the cause, and the cause of plagues is sin, if you look to it well: and the cause of sin are plays: therefore the cause of plagues are plays.

W. Thomas White, 'A sermon preached at Pawles Cross', London, 1578

SOURCE 179 **People preferred going to the theatre to going to Church**

Will not a filthy play, with the blast of a trumpet, sooner call thither a thousand than an hour's tolling of a bell bring to the sermon a hundred.

John Stockwood, 'A Sermon preached at Pawles Cross,' London, 1578

SOURCE 180 **A condemnation of plays**

Do they not maintain bawdry, insinuate foolery, and renew the remembrance of heathen idolatry? Do they not induce whoredom and uncleanness? Nay, are they not rather plain devourers of maidenly virginity and chastity? For proof whereof but

ABOVE: A contemporary painting of a mime

mark the flocking and running to Theatres and Curtains, daily and hourly, night and day, time and tide, to see plays and interludes, where such wanton gestures, such bawdy speeches, such laughing and fleering, such kissing and bussing, such clipping and culling such winking and glancing of wanton eyes, and the like is used and is wonderful to behold.

Philip Stubbes, *The Anatomie of Abuses*, 1583, F. J. Furnivall (ed.), New Shakespeare Society, 1877-79, Part I, p. 144

The theatre as a source of danger?

The theatre was regarded as a source of danger and evil for other reasons too. Pick-pockets mingled with the rest of the audience and in the large crowd there was the fear that plague might spread. This was why London theatres were closed when deaths from plague in the city reached thirty a week. Finally, there was always the danger of a riot (sources 181-186).

SOURCE 181 Theatres were unhealthy and wicked places

Plays are banished for a time out of London, lest the resort unto them should engender a plague, or rather engender it being already begun. Would to God these common plays were exiled for altogether as seminaries of impiety; and their theatres pulled down as no better than houses of bawdry.

William Harrison, *Description of England in Shakespeare's Youth*, F. J. Furnivall (ed.), New Shakespeare Society, 1877, Part I, Appendix I, p. liv

SOURCE 182 The theatre was a place of disorder

Sundry great disorders and inconveniencies have been found to ensue this city by the inordinate haunting of great multitudes of people, especially youths, to plays, interludes and shows—namely, occasions of frays and quarrels; evil practices of incontinency in great inns having chambers and secret places adjoining to their open stages and galleries . . . with drawing of the Queen's Majesty's subjects from divine service on Sundays and holidays. at which times such plays were chiefly used; unthrifty waste of the money of the poor and fond persons; sundry robberies by picking and cutting of purses . . .

'Act of the Common Council, 6 December 1574', *Collections*, Malone Society, 1908, Vol I, Part 2, p. 175

SOURCE 183 Playhouses were closed by a warrant from the Privy Council when there was an outbreak of plague

Your Lordships do permit and suffer the three Companies of Players . . . publicly to exercise their plays in their several and usual houses . . . viz the Globe situate in Maiden Lane on the Bankside in the County of Surrey, the Fortune in Golding Lane and the Curtain in Holywell in the county Middlesex without any let or interruption in respect of any former prohibition . . . Except there shall happen weekly to die of the plague above the number of thirty within the City of London and the Liberties thereof. At which time we think it fit they shall cease and forbear any further publicly to play until the sickness be again decreased to the said number.

Greg, *Henslowe's Diary*, pp. 61-2

SOURCE 184 A letter of 1597 from the Lord Mayor and Aldermen of London to the Privy Council describes the dangers of the theatre

They are the ordinary places for vagrant persons, masterless men, thieves, horse-stealers, whoremongers, cozeners, coney-catchers, contrivers of treason and other idle and dangerous persons to meet together and to make their matches to the great displeasure of Almighty God and the hurt and annoyance of her Majesty's people; which cannot be prevented nor discovered by the governors of the city for that they are out of the city's jurisdiction.

They maintain idleness in such persons as have no vocation, and draw apprentices and other servants from their ordinary works and all sorts of people from the resort unto sermons and other Christian exercises to the great hindrance of trades and profanation of religion established by her Highness within this realm.

John Dover Wilson (ed.), *Life in Shakespeare's England*, Penguin, 1968, p. 227

SOURCE 185 The Queen's godson, Harington, did not agree with the Puritans

For my part I commend not such sour censurers, but I think in stage-plays may be much good, in well-penned comedies and specially tragedies.

Harington, *Nugae Antiquae*, p. 191

ABOVE: Crowds arriving at the Globe theatre

In Augustus' time (who was the patron of all witty sports) there happened a great fray in Rome about a player, insomuch as all the city was in an uproar; whereupon the emperor (after the broil was somewhat over-blown) called the player before him and asked what was the reason that a man of his quality durst presume to make such a brawl about nothing. He smilingly replied 'It is good for thee, O Caesar, that the people's heads are troubled with brawls and quarrels about us and our light matters; for otherwise they would look into thee and thy matters'.

Thomas Nashe, *Pierce Penilesse*, 1592, London, 1924, p. 90

The audience

In spite of the dangers, and the objections of the Puritans, people of all classes flocked to the theatre to see the plays. There was a basic entrance fee of one penny for the ground area, or 'pit', and those who stood there were called the 'groundlings'. Some people could afford to pay more for a seat in the covered tiers. As such a wide range of people went to the theatre, the content of the play had to appeal to all sections of the audience. Playwrights introduced several plots and sub-plots in order to entertain everyone (sources 187-190).

LEFT: A performance in progress at the Globe theatre

SOURCE 187 People flocked to the theatres

Look but upon the common plays in London and see the multitude the flocketh to them and followeth them!

White, 'A Sermon Preached at Pawles Cross, 3 November 1577', London, 1581

SOURCE 188 The audience included people of all classes

. . . whoever cares to stand below only pays one English penny, but if he wishes to sit he enters by another door, and pays another penny, while if he desires to sit in the most comfortable seats which are cushioned, where he not only sees everything well, but can also be seen, then he pays yet another English penny at another door. And during the performance food and drink are carried round the audience, so that for what one cares to pay one may also have refreshment.

Thomas Platter, *Travels in England 1599*, Clare Williams (trans.), Jonathan Cape, 1937, p. 167

SOURCE 189 The groundlings were limited in their understanding of performances

Hamlet . . . to split the ears of the groundlings, who for the most part are capable of nothing but the inexplicable dumbshows and noise! . . .

Shakespeare, *Hamlet*, Act III, scene ii

SOURCE 190 A Puritan describes the behaviour of the audiences

Whosoever shall visit the chapel of Satan, I mean the theatre, shall find there no want of young ruffians . . . utterly past all shame . . .

A. Munday, 'A second and third blast of retreat from plays and theatres', 1580, in J. C. Adams, *The Globe Playhouse*, Harvard University Press, 1943, p. 64

ABOVE: Will Kempe

The actors

To protect themselves from being punished as vagabonds, actors banded together into companies under the protection of a prominent nobleman. Shakespeare was an actor, and a member of the company known as the Lord Chamberlain's Men (sources 191-193).

An exaggerated style of acting was common at that time, probably to help the groundlings understand what was going on, and possibly because many actors were trained in the tradition of mime and dumbshows. Shakespeare wanted his actors to be more natural in their style and reminds them through Hamlet's advice to the players (source 194).

SOURCE 191 Actors who did not have a patron were to be punished

All fences, bearwards, common players of interludes and minstrels wandering abroad (other than players of interludes belonging to any baron of this realm, or any other honourable personage of greater degree, to be authorized to play, under the hand and seal of arms of such baron or personage) . . . shall sustain such pain and punishment as by this Act is in that behalf appointed . . . Stripped naked from the middle upwards and shall be openly whipped until his or her body be bloody.
Statutes of the Realm, Vol. IV, p. 899

SOURCE 192 Shakespeare was a member of the Lord Chamberlain's Company

This comedy was first acted in the year 1598. By the then L. Chamberlain his servants. The principal comedians were:

Will. Shakespeare Ang. Phillips Hen. Condell Will. Sly Will. Kempe Ric. Burbage Joh. Hemings Rho. Pope Chr. Beeston Joh. Duke
Ben Jonson, *Every Man in His Humour*, Folio edition, London, 1616, title page

SOURCE 193 A royal licence for Shakespeare's company The King's Players, May 19, 1603

James by the Grace of God etc. To all justices, mayors, sheriffs, constables, headboroughs and other our officers and loving subjects greeting. Know ye that we of our special grace, certain knowledge and mere motion, have licensed and authorized and by these presents do license and authorize these our servants, Lawrence Fletcher, William

Shakespeare, Richard Burbage, Augustine Phillipps, John Heming, Henry Condell, William Sly, Robert Armin, Richard Cowley, and the rest of their associates freely to use and exercise the art and faculty of playing comedies, tragedies, histories, interludes, morals, pastorals, stage-plays, and such other like as they have already studied or hereafter shall use or study, as well for the recreation of our loving subjects as for our solace and pleasure when we shall think good to see them during our pleasure.

SOURCE 194 Hamlet's advice to the players

Hamlet. Speak the speech, I pray you, as I pronounced it to you, trippingly on the tongue; but if you mouth it, as many of your players do, I had as lief the town-crier spoke my lines. Nor do not saw the air too much with your hand, thus, but use all gently; for in the very torrent, tempest, and, as I may say, the whirlwind of passion, you must acquire and beget a temperance that may give it smoothness. O, it offends me to the soul to see a robustious periwig-pated fellow tear a passion to tatters . . .

Shakespeare, *Hamlet*, Act III, scene ii

BELOW: Richard Burbage

Leading actors of the time

The leading tragic actor of Shakespeare's company was Richard Burbage, who came from a family with strong links with the theatre. He played all Shakespeare's tragic heroes—Romeo, Hamlet, Othello, Lear and Macbeth. His reputation was such that even years after his death a writer described his acting in glowing terms (source 195).

The company had two principal comedians. One was Will Kempe, who was famous for his clowning. He played parts such as Bottom in *A Midsummer Night's Dream*, Launcelot in *The Merchant of Venice* and Dogberry in *Much Ado About Nothing*. It is generally supposed that Shakespeare had him in mind when he made Hamlet refer to clowns who disrupt the action of the play (source 196). The other comedian was Thomas Pope. No doubt he grew to be a fat man, for he played the parts of Falstaff and Sir Toby Belch.

Women's parts were played by boys. To make them credible as women Shakespeare used a number of devices. Frequently he caused his heroines to disguise themselves as boys. This enabled the boy actors to behave more naturally. To persuade the audience that the boy on stage was really a beautiful woman, he placed exaggerated descriptions in the mouths of the other characters (sources 197-199).

SOURCE 195 Richard Burbage was much better than the general run of actors

. . . he was a delightful Proteus, so wholly transforming himself into his part, and putting off himself with his clothes, as he never (not so much as in the tiring house) assumed himself again until the play was done: there being as much difference between him and one of our common actors, as between a ballad singer who only mouths it, and an excellent singer, who knows all his graces, and can artfully vary and modulate his voice, even to know how much breath he is to give to every syllable.

Richard Flecknoe, 'A Short Discourse of the English Stage', 1664, in A. M. Nagler, *A Source Book in Theatrical History*, Dover Publications, 1959, p. 128

SOURCE 196 Shakespeare had difficulty in making his clowns stick to the words written for them

Hamlet . . . And let those that play your clowns speak no more than is set down for them; for there be of them that will themselves laugh, to set on some quantity of barren spectators to laugh too, though in the mean time, some necessary question of the play be then to be considered: . . .

Shakespeare, *Hamlet*, Act III, scene ii

SOURCE 197 The women in Shakespeare's plays frequently dressed up as boys

Portia. Come on Nerissa; I have work in hand
  That you yet know not of; we'll see our husbands
  Before they think of us!
Nerissa. Shall they see us?
Portia. They shall, Nerissa; but in such a habit,
  That they shall think we are accomplished
  With that we lack.   I'll hold thee any wager,
  When we are both accoutred like young men,
  I'll prove the prettier fellow of the two,
  And wear my dagger with the braver grace,
  And speak between the change of man and boy
  With a reed voice, and turn two mincing steps
  Into a manly stride . . .

William Shakespeare, *Merchant of Venice*, Act III, scene iv

SOURCE 198 The text of the play persuades the audience that the boy actor is a beautiful woman

Enobarbus. For her own person,
  It beggar'd all description: she did lie
  In her pavilion, cloth-of-gold of tissue—
  O'er picturing that Venus where we see
  The fancy outwork Nature . . .

William Shakespeare, *Anthony and Cleopatra*, Act II, scene ii

SOURCE 199 Theatres in London and Venice compared by an English traveller

I was at one of their play-houses, where I saw a comedy acted. The house is very beggarly and base in comparison of our stately play-houses in England: neither can their actors compare with us for apparel, shews and music. Here I observed certain things that I never saw before. For I saw women act, a thing that I never saw before, though I have heard that it hath been sometimes used in London; and they performed it with as good a grace, action, gesture, and whatsoever convenient for a player, as ever I saw a masculine actor.

Thomas Coryat, *Crudities*, London, 1611, p. 247

BELOW: Aristocratic members of the audience

The English Renaissance

Shakespeare's poetry and drama represent the height of the Renaissance achievement in England. It is not surprising that the interests of the age are reflected in his plays. Many of them are set in Italy, the centre of Renaissance learning and discuss new ideas brought back from Europe. There are also several references to exotic places and to rich materials and luxurious food and drink which Elizabethan travellers brought to England for the first time.

Shakespeare also reflected the great love of music which the Elizabethans had, by using music in many of his plays.

At the same time the age was one of superstition and cruelty. Many people were afraid of witches and those who were suspected of witch-craft were executed. Punishments for all kinds of crimes were severe. Many of the pastimes in which people indulged showed a delight in violence and bloodshed. These characteristics are all reflected in the plays that were written and performed at this time. One of the most important factors in the English Renaissance was the new found confidence and pride in England and her accomplishments (source 200).

ABOVE: Ben Jonson with friends in the Devil Tavern

SOURCE 200 Shakespeare expressed the pride and confidence that people felt for their country

Gaunt. . . .This royal throne of kings, this sceptred isle,
  This earth of majesty, this seat of Mars,
  This other Eden, demi-paradise,
  This fortress built by nature for herself
  Against infection and the hand of war,
  This happy breed of men, this little world,
  This precious stone set in the silver sea,
  Or as a moat defensive to a house,
  Against the envy of less happier lands
  This blessed plot, this earth, this realm, this England . . .

William Shakespeare, *Richard II*, Act II, scene i

6
Ships and seamen

By 1588, England was one of the greatest naval powers in the world. Her ships were better designed than those of Spain, her greatest rival. English sailors were unsurpassed for skill and daring both in war and peacetime conditions (source 201).

Yet this had not always been the case. In the fifteenth century and the early years of the sixteenth century, it had been the Spanish and Portuguese sailors who led the way in voyages of exploration. They established settlements in Africa, Asia and America. The Pope acknowledged their right to a monopoly of trade with these newly discovered countries (source 202).

English enterprise began in the late fifteenth century and gathered pace from the 1550s. In 1553, Willoughby and Chancellor tried to find a new trade route to the east, a passage round the north-east of Europe to China. Soon after that, men such as Thomas Wyndham,

John Lok and William Towerson explored the west coast of Africa. These, and other voyages, aroused interest in the achievements of the Portuguese and Spaniards. Books were written about geography and navigation. Englishmen were encouraged by the thought of making money from trading voyages to the new countries (sources 203-208).

BELOW: Spanish shipbuilding plans, 1587

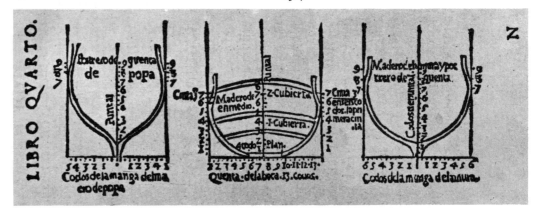

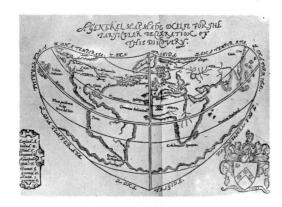

ABOVE: Sir Humphrey Gilbert's map
of the world, 1576

SOURCE 201 The achievements of English sailors

. . . to speak a word of that just commendation which our nation do indeed deserve: it cannot be denied, but as in all former ages, they have been men full of activity, stirrers abroad, and searchers of remote parts of the world, so in this most famous and peerless government of her most excellent Majesty, her subjects through the special assistance and blessing of God, in searching the most opposite corners and quarters of the world and to speak plainly, in compassing the vast globe of the earth more than once, have excelled all the nations and people of the earth. For, which of the kings of this land before her Majesty, had their banners ever seen in the Caspian Sea? Which of them hath ever dealt with the Emperor of Persia, as her Majesty hath done and obtained for her merchants large and loving privileges? Who ever saw, before this regiment, an English leger in the stately porch of the Grand Signor at Constantinople? Who ever found English consuls and agents at Tripolis, in Syria, at Aleppo, at Babylon, at Balsara, and which is more, who ever heard of Englishmen at Goa before now? What ships did heretofore ever anchor in the mighty river of Plate? . . . and return home most richly laden with the commodities of China, as the subjects of this now flourishing monarchy have done?

Richard Hakluyt, *The Principal Navigations Voyages Traffiques and Discoveries of the English Nation*, 1589, Glasgow, 1903-4, p. xx

SOURCE 202 The world is divided between Spain and Portugal

. . . in 1494, [John II, King of Portugal] concluded the Treaty of Tordesillas with them [King Ferdinand and Queen Isabella of Spain]. By this treaty, which was confirmed by a Bull, issued by Pope Alexander VI, the limits of the future possessions of the Spaniards and Portuguese in the regions discovered and explored by their mariners was fixed at 360° east of Cape Verde, and it was agreed that the Spaniards were to have full right to all lands discovered to the west of this line, and the Portuguese to all to the south and east.

H. Morse Stephens, *Portugal*, T. Fisher Unwin, 1891, pp. 163-4

SOURCE 203 In 1583 it was argued that the example of Spain and Portugal should stimulate English enterprise

To what end need I endeavour myself by arguments to prove that by this voyage our navy and navigation shall be enlarged, when as there needeth none other reason than the manifest example of the near neighbours to this realm, the Kings of Spain and Portugal, who, since the first discovery of the Indies, have not only mightily enlarged their dominions, greatly enriched themselves and their subjects, but have also, by just account, trebled the number of their ships, masters and mariners, a matter of no small moment and importance?

Hakluyt, *Principal Navigations*, Vol. VIII, 1599-60, p. 111-12

SOURCE 204 Reasons why English sailors should seek a north-east passage to the far east

Whereas the Portingals have, in their course to the Indies in the Southeast, certain ports and fortifications to thrust into by the way . . . so you are to see what Islands, and what ports you need to have by the way in your course to the Northeast . . . And for that the people to the which we purpose in this voyage to go be no Christians, it were good that the means of our commodities were always in our own disposition, and not at the will of others.

Hakluyt, *Principal Navigations*, Vol. III, p. 264

SOURCE 205 Reasons why English colonies should be planted in North America

. . . it is very certain that the greatest . . . strength of this realm for defence and offence in martial matters . . . is the multitude of ships, masters and mariners, ready to assist the most stately and royal navy of her Majesty, which by reason of this voyage shall have both increase and maintenance. And it is well known that in sundry places of this realm ships have been built . . . for the trade of fishing only . . . If our nation were once planted there [North America], or near thereabouts; whereas they now fish but for two months of the year, they might then fish so long as pleased themselves.

Hakluyt, *Principal Navigations*, Vol. VIII, p. 110

ABOVE: Sir Humphrey Gilbert, explorer

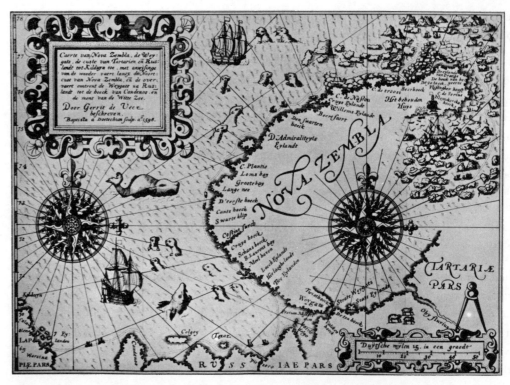

SOURCE 206 English trade would benefit from voyages to America and the far east

. . . it is well known that all Savages, as well these that dwell in the South, as those that dwell in the North, so soon as they shall begin but a little to taste of civility, will take marvellous delight in any garment, be it never so simple; as a shirt, a blue, yellow, red, or green cotton cassock, a cap, or such like, and will take incredible pains for such a trifle.

. . . what vent for our English clothes will thereby ensure, and how great benefit to all such persons and artificers [Clothiers, Woolmen, Carders, Spinners, Weavers, Fullers etc.] I do leave to the judgement of such as are discreet.

Hakluyt, *Principal Navigations*, Vol. VIII, p. III

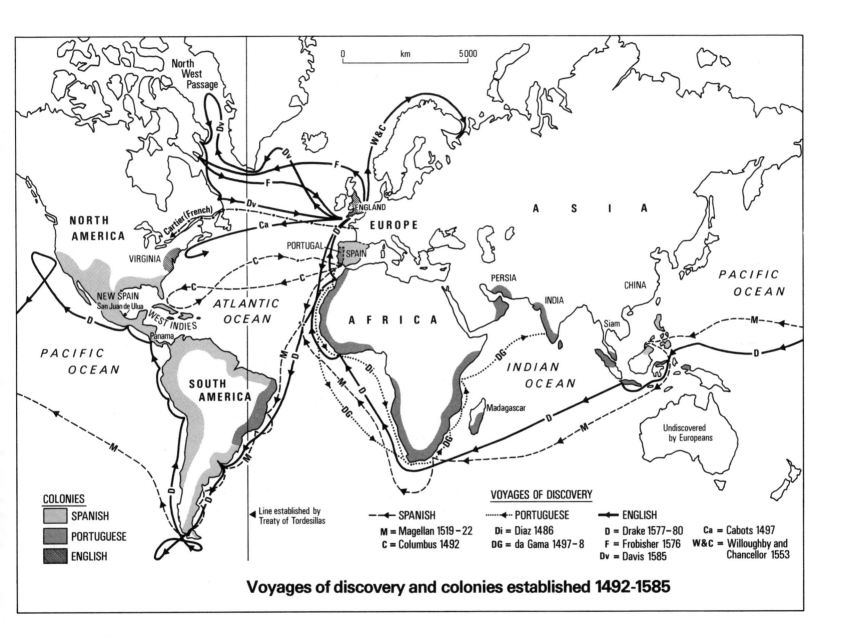

Voyages of discovery and colonies established 1492-1585

North West Passage

NORTH AMERICA

ENGLAND

EUROPE

ASIA

PACIFIC OCEAN

Cartier (French)

VIRGINIA

NEW SPAIN
San Juan de Ulua

WEST INDIES

Panama

PORTUGAL

SPAIN

PERSIA

INDIA

CHINA

Siam

PACIFIC OCEAN

ATLANTIC OCEAN

AFRICA

PACIFIC OCEAN

SOUTH AMERICA

INDIAN OCEAN

Madagascar

Undiscovered by Europeans

COLONIES
SPANISH
PORTUGUESE
ENGLISH

◄ Line established by Treaty of Tordesillas

VOYAGES OF DISCOVERY

– ◄ – SPANISH
········► PORTUGUESE
——► ENGLISH

M = Magellan 1519–22
C = Columbus 1492

Di = Diaz 1486
DG = da Gama 1497–8

D = Drake 1577–80
F = Frobisher 1576
Dv = Davis 1585

Ca = Cabots 1497
W&C = Willoughby and Chancellor 1553

SOURCE 207 Increased trade would provide work for the unemployed

. . . it will prove a general benefit unto our country that, not only a great number of men which do now live idly at home and are a burden, chargeable and unprofitable to this realm, shall hereby be set to work, but also children of twelve or fourteen years of age, or older, may be kept from idleness, in making of a thousand kinds of trifling things which will be good merchandize for that country. And, moreover, our idle women (which the Realm may well spare) shall also be employed on plucking, drying, and sorting of feathers, in pulling, beating, and working of hemp, and in gathering of cotton, and divers things right necessary for dyeing.

Hakluyt, *Principal Navigations*, Vol. VIII, p. 112

SOURCE 208 The benefits the English voyages would bring to the 'savages'

. . . this voyage is not altogether undertaken for the peculiar commodity of ourselves and our country . . . [but] the Savages shall have cause to bless the hour when this enterprise was undertaken.

First and chiefly, in respect of the most happy and gladsome tidings of the most glorious Gospel of our Saviour, Jesus Christ, whereby they may be brought from falsehood to truth . . .

. . . being brought from brutish ignorance to civility and knowledge, and made to understand how the tenth part of their land may be so manured and employed, as it may yield more commodities to the necessary use of man's life, than the whole now doth . . .

But this is not all the benefit which they shall receive; for over and beside the knowledge how to till and dress their grounds, they shall be reduced from unseemly customs to honest manners, from disordered riotous routs to a well governed common wealth . . .

Hakluyt, *Principal Navigations*, Vol. VIII, pp. 119-20

Sir John Hawkins

Sir John Hawkins was one of the first Englishmen to try to break the Portuguese and Spanish monopoly. In 1562, and again in 1564, he sailed to the west coast of Africa, captured a large party of negro slaves and transported them to South America, where he sold them at great profit. On his third voyage, however, in 1567, there occurred an event that was to mark the break in the peaceful trading relations between England and Spain. Hawkins's party suffered a surprise attack from a Spanish fleet in San Juan de Ulua harbour in Mexico (source 209).

Henceforth English seamen regarded Spain as an enemy. Her treasure ships were the prize they sought in their revenge for that attack. In the struggle that developed in the following years, the name that the Spaniards came to fear most was that of Drake.

SOURCE 209 The Spanish betrayal at San Juan de Ulua

. . . there happened to us the 12th day of August [1567] an extreme storm which continued by the space of 4 days, which so beat the Jesus, that we cut down all her higher buildings, her rudder also was sore shaken, and withal was in so extreme a leak . . . we were forced to make for the port which serveth the City of Mexico called St John de Ulua . . . [On 16th September] we saw outside the haven 13 great ships, and understanding them to be the fleet of Spain, I sent immediately to advertise the General of the fleet of my being there, doing him to understand, that before I would suffer them to enter the Port, there should some other order of conditions pass between us for our safe being there, and maintenance of peace . . . the Viceroy signed with his hand and sealed with his seal of all the conditions concluded, and forthwith a trumpet blown

ABOVE: Sir Francis Drake, c. 1580

with commandment that none of either party should inviolate the peace upon pain of death . . .

. . . the next Thursday, being the 23 of September, at dinner time [the Spaniards] blew the trumpet, and from all sides set upon us . . .

John Hawkins, 'The Third Voyage of Sir John Hawkins', in C. R. Markham (ed.), *The Hawkins' Voyages During the Reigns of Henry VIII, Queen Elizabeth and James I*, Hakluyt Society, 1878, pp. 73-4

Drake's voyage of discovery

Drake's most famous voyage was his circumnavigation of the world between 1577 and 1580. A detailed study of that voyage will show not only what type of man he was but also the sort of experiences that were to make English seamen supreme. Fortunately, many accounts have survived from those who sailed with him and from others whom he captured.

Motives

The voyage began in some secrecy, although it was generally understood that it was to be a long voyage. Drake was later to claim that he undertook the voyage on the Queen's orders but he made no secret of the fact that he was seeking revenge for the attack at San Juan de Ulua (sources 210-214).

SOURCE 210 At the beginning of the voyage details were kept secret

They left Plymouth towards the end of December and [John Drake] went in the Captain's ship, serving Captain Francis as page. [John] understood that when they left England there were not two men in the fleet who knew whihter they were bound . . .

'Second Declaration of John Drake' in Z. Nuttall (ed.), *New Light on Drake: A Collection of Documents Relating to His Voyage of Circumnavigation 1577-1580*, Hakluyt Society Series II, Vol. 34, 1914, p. 36

SOURCE 211 It was generally understood that it was to be long voyage.

. . . after the taking of the said ship he, the said Drake, did put the men aland in a pinnace and carried away the wines with the ship for the relief and maintenance of himself and company being bent upon a long voyage of two years as he said, and as it was then supposed . . .

'Declaration of John Winter', 1579, in Nuttall, *New Light on Drake*, pp. 386-7

SOURCE 212 Drake consistently argued that he was seeking revenge for San Juan de Ulua

. . . the Queen, my Sovereign Lady, has ordered me to come to these parts. It is thus that I am acting, and if it is wrong it is she who knows best and I am not to be blamed for anything whatsoever. But I do regret to possess myself of anything that does not belong exclusively to King Philip or to Don Martin Enriquez, for it grieves me that their vassals should be paying for them. But I am not going to stop until I have collected the two millions that my cousin, John Hawkins, lost, for certain, at San Juan de Ulua

'Deposition of the Factor of Guatulco', 1580, in Nuttall, *New Light on Drake*, p. 357

SOURCE 213 Drake again asserts that he is seeking revenge

. . . they ordered me to go in their boat to where their general [Drake] was . . . [he] asked me if I knew your Excellency [Don Martin Enriquez, Viceroy of New Spain], I said, "yes". "Is any relative of his or thing pertaining to him on this ship?". "No, sir". "Well, it would give me a great joy to come across him than all the gold and silver of the Indies. You would see how the words of gentlemen should be kept".

'Testimony of Francisco de Zarate', 1579, in Nuttall, *New Light on Drake*, pp. 202-3

SOURCE 214 Further evidence that Drake was exacting revenge for the attack at San Juan de Ulua

Francis Drake complained of the Viceroy of Mexico, [Don Martin Enriquez] saying that he had broken his word to John Hawkins and had not observed the King of Spain's warrant of safety. Francis Drake stated that he had been present and had lost seven thousand pesos in that defeat and that three hundred Englishmen had been killed.

He added that for the reason that the King had, since that time, been his treasurer for the sum that had been taken from him ten years ago, he now wished to act as treasurer of the King's estate. Therefore the silver which he took from the King was for himself; the silver taken from private individuals was for his Queen, his Sovereign Lady.

'Testimony of San Juan de Anton', 1579, in Nuttall, *New Light on Drake*, p. 161

ABOVE: Drake's ship, the *Pelican*, renamed the *Golden Hind*

His ships

His fleet consisted of five small ships. Their ability to withstand weather conditions was tested as soon as they left port. A storm sprang up on the very night that they set sail. The damage they suffered forced them to put back into harbour for repairs (sources 215, 216).

SOURCE 215 Drake's fleet for his voyage round the world

. . . with the help of divers friends adventurers, he had fitted himself with five ships.

1. The *Pelican*, admiral, burthen 100 tons, Captain-General Francis Drake
2. The *Elizabeth*, vice-admiral, burthen 80 tons, Captain John Winter
3. The *Marigold*, a bark of 30 tons, Captain John Thomas
4. The *Swan*, a flyboat of 50 tons, Captain John Chester
5. The *Christopher*, a pinnace of 15 tons, Captain Thomas Moone

These ships he manned with 164 able and sufficient men, and furnished them also with such plentiful provision of all things necessary, as so long and dangerous a voyage did seem to require . . .

Sir Francis Drake, *The World Encompassed*, Hakluyt Society, 1854, pp. 6-7

SOURCE 216 The voyage began badly

Being thus appointed, we set sail out of the South of Plymouth, about 5 of the clock in the afternoon, November 15, of the same year [1577], and running all that night Southwest, by the morning were come as far as the Lizard, where meeting the wind at Southwest (quite contrary to our intended course), we were forced, with our whole fleet, to put into Falmouth.

The next day towards evening, there arose a storm, continuing all that night and the day following . . . with such violence, that though it were in a very good harbour, yet 2 of our ships, viz the Admiral and the Marigold, were fain to cut their main masts by board, and for the repairing of them, and many other damages in the tempest sustained . . . to bear back to Plymouth again, where we all arrived the 13th day after our departure thence.

Drake, *The World*, pp. 7-8

The mutiny

So great were their fears of the dangers they faced during the voyage that the crew rebelled. The leader of the mutiny was Thomas Doughty. Drake set up a court on board ship. Doughty was tried, found guilty and executed (sources 217-220).

ABOVE: An Elizabethan pinnace

SOURCE 217 The expedition faced dangers on land as well as on sea

From thence he went to the island of Mocha which is inhabited by Indians, and landed to get water; but the Indians attacked him and killed his pilot and surgeon and wounded nine or ten. The chief was wounded by arrows, one of which entered his head, the other his face. There was one man who received twenty-five arrow wounds, another twenty-three.

'Narrative of Pedro Sarmiento', 1579, in Nuttall, *New Light on Drake*, p. 65

SOURCE 218 An account of the trial of Thomas Doughty for mutiny

The last day of June, [1578] the General [Drake] himself being set in place of judgment . . . spoke unto Master Thomas Doughty, who then was brought hither more like a prisoner than a gentleman, "Thomas Doughty, you have here sought by divers means to discredit me, to the great hindrance and overthrow of this voyage . . . if you can clear yourself, you and I shall be very good friends, but if the contrary, you have deserved death . . ."

Then, was there a Jury called, where of Master John Winter was foreman . . . Master Doughty said that my Lord Treasurer had a plot [the details] of the voyage. "No, that he hath not", said Master Drake. The other replied that he had. "How?" asked Master Drake. "He had it from me" said Master Doughty. "Lo, my masters", said he, "what this fellow hath done, God will have his treacheries all known, for her Majesty gave me special commandment that of all men my Lord Treasurer should not know it. But see, his own mouth hath betrayed him. So this was a special article against him, to cut his throat . . ."

So with this the Jury went together, finding all to be true . . .

Drake, *The World*, pp. 203-4

SOURCE 219 The execution of Thomas Doughty

They [Drake and Doughty] having thus received the sacrament there was a Banquet made such as the place might yield, and there they dined together, in which time the place of execution being made ready, after dinner, as one not willing any longer to delay the time, [he] told the General that he was ready as soon as it pleased him . . . then with bills and staves he was brought to the place of execution where he showed himself no less valiant than all the time before, for first here kneeling on his knees, he prayed for the queen's majesty of England [and] prayed to God for the happy success of this voyage . . .

So then Master Doughty, embracing the General, bade him farewell, and so bidding the whole company farewell, he laid his head to the block, the which being stricken off, Drake . . . made the head to be taken up and shewed to the whole company, himself saying, lo, this is the end of traitors.

Drake , *The World*, pp. 208-10

SOURCE 220 Why was Doughty executed?

. . . one of the gentlemen [Thomas Doughty], whom he had with him, said to him: "We have been a long while in this strait and you have placed all of us, who follow or serve you, in danger of death. It would therefore be prudent for you to give order that we return to the North Sea, where we have the certainty of capturing prizes, and that we give up seeking to make new discoveries. You see how fraught with difficulties these are".

This gentleman [Doughty] must have sustained this opinion with more vigour than appeared proper to the General [Drake]. His answer was that he had the gentleman carried below deck and put in irons. On another day, at the same hour, he ordered him to be taken out, and to be beheaded in the presence of all.

Nuttall, *New Light on Drake*, p. 208

Drake as a captain

Drake had a reputation as a strict disciplinarian but he looked after his men and was well-liked by them. He was physically strong and survived being wounded on more than one occasion. He lived in the style of a nobleman on board ship. His prisoners reported that he was courteous to them and did not compel them to follow his own Puritan form of worship (sources 221-226).

SOURCE 221 Drake was a strict disciplinarian

. . . all [his crew] are of an age for warfare, and all are as practised therein as old soldiers from Italy could be. Each one takes particular pains to keep his arquebuse clean. He treats them with affection, and they treat him with respect. [The cadets] form a part of his council which he calls together for even the most trivial matter, although he takes advice from no one, but he enjoys hearing what they say and afterwards issues his orders. He has no favourite.

. . . I understand that all the men he carries with him receive wages . . . He shows them great favour, but punishes the least fault.

'Testimony of Francisco de Zarate', 1579, in Nuttall, *New Light on Drake*, p. 207

SOURCE 222 One of Drake's Spanish captives reports the crew's opinions of him

I managed to ascertain whether the General [Francis Drake] was well liked, and all said that they adored him.

'Testimony of Francisco de Zarate', 1579, in Nuttall, *New Light on Drake*, p. 209

SOURCE 223 A Portuguese captive's description of Francis Drake

This Englishman calls himself Francis Drake and is a man aged 38. He may be two years more or less. He is low in stature, thick-set and very robust. He has a fine countenance, is ruddy of complexion and has a fair beard. He has the mark of an arrow-wound in his right cheek which is not apparent if one does not look with special care. In one leg he has the ball of an arquebuse that was shot at him in the Indies. He is a great mariner . . .

'Nuno da Silva's sworn deposition', 1579, in Nuttall, *New Light on Drake*, p. 301

BELOW: A Mariner's mirror, 1586

SOURCE 224 Drake lived in style on board his ship

His vessel is a galleon of nearly four hundred tons, and is a perfect sailer. She is manned with a hundred men, . . . He carries with him nine or ten cavaliers, cadets of English Noblemen . . .

The aforesaid gentlemen sit at his table, as well as a Portuguese pilot, whom he brought from England, who spoke not a word during all the time I was on board. He is served on silver dishes with gold borders and gilded garlands, in which are his arms. He carries all possible dainties and perfumed waters. He said that many of these had been given him by the Queen.

'Testimony of Francisco de Zarate', 1579, in Nuttall, *New Light on Drake*, p. 207

SOURCE 225 Drake was courteous to his captive

Of that which belonged to me he took but little. Indeed he was quite courteous about it. Certain, trifles of mine having taken his fancy, he had them brought to his ship and gave me, in exchange for them, a falchion and a small brazier of silver, and I can assure your Excellency that he lost nothing by the bargain. On his return to his vessel he asked me to pardon him for taking the trifles, but they were for his wife.

The next morning, which was Monday, he gave back to some of the passengers who were there, their boxes, and thus occupied himself until the hour for dinner . . . having all our sailors called together, he gave each one handful of reals. He also gave the same to some other men who appeared to him to be the most needy.

'Testimony of Francisco de Zarate', 1579, in Nuttall, *New Light on Drake*, pp. 204–5

SOURCE 226 Drake leads his men in worship

. . . Francis Drake had a table placed on deck at the poop of the vessel, and, at its head on the floor, a small box and an embroidered cushion. He then sent for a book of the Lives of the Saints and when all this was in place he struck the table twice with the palm of his hand. Then, immediately nine Englishmen, with nine small books of the size of a breviary, joined him and seated themselves around him and the table. Then the said Francis Drake crossed his hands and, kneeling on the cushions and small box, lifted his eyes to heaven and remained in that attitude for about a quarter of an hour.

He then said to this witness and to the other prisoners that if they wanted to recite the psalms according to his mode they could stay, but if not, that they could go to the prow. As they stood up to go towards the prow, he spoke saying "that they were to keep quiet", and he began reading the psalms in the English language of which witness understood nothing whatsoever. This act lasted about an hour and then they brought four viols, and made lamentations and sang together, with the accompaniment of the stringed instruments. Witness does not know what they sang, as he could not understand it.

Immediately afterwards he ordered a boy, whom he had brought as a page, to come and then made him dance in the English fashion, with which the service ended.

'Deposition of the Factor of Guatalco', 1580, in Nuttall, *New Light on Drake*, pp. 354-5

Rewards of the voyage

During their voyage, Drake and his men attacked Spanish ships and ports, collecting a rich booty and earning themselves a fearsome reputation. They also learned and practised the skills of seamanship and gunnery that helped them to defeat the Spanish Armada (sources 227-231).

SOURCE 227 Drake attacks a Spanish ship

At about nine o'clock at night, the English ship crossed the course of San Juan's vessel and, immediately, came alongside. San Juan saluted but the Corsair did not return the salute . . . Master de Anton came to the side. By that time the English were already grappling his ship shouting: "Englishmen! strike sail!" Someone said: "Strike sail, Mr Juan de Anton; if not, look out, for you will be sent to the bottom".

San Juan answered: "What England is this [which gives me orders] for striking sail? Come on board to strike [the] sails yourselves!" On hearing this they blew a whistle on the English ship and the trumpet responded. Then a volley of what seemed to be about sixty arquebuses was shot, followed by many arrows, which struck the side of the ship, and chain balls shot from a heavy piece of ordinance carried away the mizen and sent it into the sea with its sail and lateen yard. After this the English shot another great gun, shouting again "Strike sail!" and, simultaneously, a pinnace laid aboard to port and about forty archers climbed up the channels of the shrouds and entered San Juan de Anton's ship, while, at the opposite side, the English ship laid aboard. It is thus

ABOVE: "A moveable compass of the stars", 1586

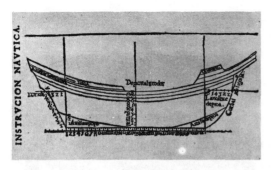

ABOVE: Spanish shipbuilding plan, 1587

that they forced San Juan's ship to surrender. They inquired for the pilot and captain from the self-same San Juan de Anton, who was alone on deck. He would not answer them. Not seeing any other person on deck, they seized him and carried him to the English ship 'where he saw the Corsair Francis Drake, who was removing his helmet and coat of mail. Francis Drake embraced San Juan de Anton, saying "Have patience, for such is the usage of war", and immediately ordered him to be locked up in the cabin in the poop, with twelve men to guard him.

'Testimony of San Juan de Anton', 1579, in Nuttall, *New Light on Drake*, pp. 156-8

SOURCE 228 Drake attacks a port

In the month of April in the previous year of 1579 on Monday of Holy Week on the thirteenth day of the month and about noontime two vessels entered this port. One was large; the other was a small frigate. On seeing them, this witness wanted to visit them . . . Just then a boat left the vessel, with apparently twenty or twenty-five men, and came ashore in great haste with the frigate. It was not known who they were until they were so close to land that they could almost leap ashore.

No one, at the time, knew who they were until a sailor cried out "The English, the English!" This witness then summoned, in the King's [Philip II] name the few Spaniards who were about, and went to the market-place of the said port, so as to protect the land. This had, however, little effect on account of the number of Englishmen who jumped ashore from the frigate and boat, armed with arquebuses, swords and shields. On their account and because some pieces of artillery were shot from the said frigate, not a person remained with this witness, who therefore retired, little by little until he reached the wood at about 50 or 100 paces from the church of this port. There he remained for the space of three or four hours during which the said Englishman sacked the port.

There this witness returned to the church, which he found robbed of its sacred vestments, which were many and good. The picture that was on the altar was destroyed and cut; the bell had been stolen and offences and sacrileges had been committed such as the said English would naturally do, being as they were, Lutheran heretics.

They had taken prisoners . . . [who] were kept on his ship until Holy Tuesday, when at four o'clock in the afternoon, he sent them ashore. From these men witness learnt that the captain of that vessel and the frigate was named Francis Drake . . . [he] remained over Wednesday and Thursday robbing merchandise from a vessel that was about to leave this port for Zonzonate. On Good Friday, before daybreak, he set sail . . .

'Deposition of the Alcalde of Guatulco', 1580, in Nuttall, *New Light on Drake*, pp. 340-1

SOURCE 229 Rough justice for the captives

[Drake] continued his voyage, and on the 27th of February, at night, took another ship bound for Panama and laden with provisions for the King's vessels, with two thousand bags and other things and with 40 bars of silver and gold. And because a sailor secretly took a bar of gold and did not declare it, he hanged him and let the ship go.

'Nuno da Silva's first relation', 1579, in Nuttall, *New Light on Drake*, p. 249

SOURCE 230 The man who was 'hanged' tells his own story

[Francisco Jacome] saw that the Englishmen, like men whose profession is warfare, carried many arquebuses and all kinds of arms. On the day after seizing them, the Englishmen took out the said pieces of artillery which they had placed in the ship on which [Jacome] came.

. . . the said Englishmen returned in a launch and carried him back to their said ship and waited to hang him, demanding from him the gold which they said he had concealed in the ship. As [Jacome] had not hidden anything whatsoever and was unable to reveal anything to them, they hanged him by the neck with a cord as though to hang him outright, and let him drop from high into the sea, from which they fetched him out with the launch and took him back to the ship on which he had come. It was thus that he parted from them.

'Deposition of Francisco Jacome', 1578, in Nuttall, *New Light on Drake*, p. 151

SOURCE 231 The quantity of Drake's booty

1. Tremayne's official return of what he sent up to the Tower from Saltash Castle . . . shows forty-six parcels of treasure averaging over 2 cwt. each i.e. nearly five tons. The exact amount registered was 4 tons, 15 cwt. 4 lbs. This was after Drake had been

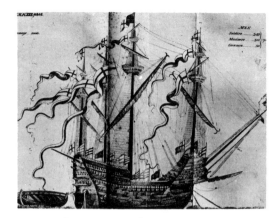

ABOVE: The *Harry Grace à Dieu*, or *Great Harry* built for Henry VIII

authorised secretly to abstract a large amount for himself and his crew, besides several horse-loads of gold and silver, and some of the most precious items of his booty, which John Drake says he himself took with him to London.

2. Another account of all silver bullion that was brought into the Tower by Sir Francis Drake, dated December 26 1585, . . . puts the total at over 10 tons.

The figures are as follows:

	lbs.	ozs.
650 ingots of silver fine and coarse	22 899	5
Sundry pieces of 'corrento' coarse	512	6
Total	23 411	11

J. S. Corbett, *Drake and the Tudor Navy*, Longmans, Green & Co., 1899, Vol. I, Appendix F, pp. 408-9

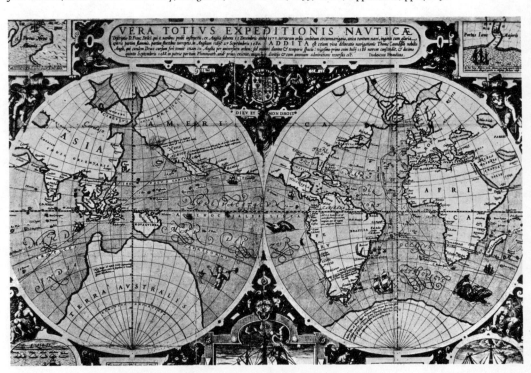

RIGHT: Contemporary map showing Drake's circumnavigation of the world and some later voyages

Conditions on ship

The hardiness of the men may be judged from the conditions in which they were forced to live. Not only were conditions cramped and unhealthy, but food supplies were of poor quality and quantity. While the Royal Navy was patrolling the Channel in 1588 to intercept the Armada, an infection swept through one of the ships, the *Jonas Elizabeth*. The sailors' resistance was low and it quickly spread to the remaining ships (sources 232-234).

SOURCE 232 Infection aboard ship is described by Howard in a letter to Burghley dated 10 August 1588

Sickness and mortality begins wonderfully to grow amongst us . . . The *Jonas Elizabeth*, which hath done as well as ever any ship did in any service, hath had a great infection in her from the beginning so as of the 500 men which she carried out, by the time she had been in Plymouth three weeks or a month there were dead of them 200 and above, so as I was driven to set all the rest of her men ashore, to take out the ballast and to make fires in her of wet broom 3 or 4 days together, and so hoped thereby to have cleaned her of her infection, and thereupon got new men, very tall and able as ever I saw and put them into her; now the infection is broken out in greater extremity than ever it did before, and they die and sicken faster then ever they did . . . Sir Roger Townsend of all the men he brought with him hath but one left alive . . . it is like enough that the like infection will grow throughout the most part of the fleet for they have been so long at sea and have so little shift of apparel . . .

H. W. Hodges & E. A. Hughes (eds.), *Select Naval Documents*, Cambridge University Press, 1936, pp. 29-30

SOURCE 233 Howard reports to the Privy Council in 1588 that the seamen were short of food

My Lords our victuals are not yet come, but we hope shortly to hear of them . . . If they come not, our extremity will be very great . . . Several men have fallen sick, and by thousands fain to be discharged . . .

Hodges, *Select Naval Documents*, pp. 17-18

SOURCE 234 The provisions issued to the seamen were bad

The beer brewed at Sandwich was sour . . . The mariners think it was one great cause of infection. Nothing displeaseth them more than to have sour beer.

Green, *State Papers, Domestic*, 1581-1590, p. 536

BELOW: Lord Howard of Effingham, Admiral of the Fleet

ABOVE: The *Ark Royal*

The Armada and English seapower

The victory over the Spanish Armada marked a turning point in Elizabeth's reign. It did not end the war. Fighting continued for almost another twenty years. But the triumph of the seamen in 1588 was also a triumph for English naval tactics and skills in warfare (sources 235, 236). It gave Englishmen great confidence; ships ventured into every part of the world on voyages of discovery, trade and piracy (sources 237-240).

SOURCE 235 Raleigh's instructions, 1617, on English naval tactics

If we find an enemy to be leewards of us, the whole fleet shall follow the admiral, vice-admiral, or other leading ship within musket shot of the enemy; giving so much liberty to the leading ship as after her broadside she may stay and trim her sails. Then is the second ship to take as the first ship and give the other side, keeping the enemy under perpetual shot. This you must do upon the windermost ship or ships of an enemy which you shall either batter in pieces, or force him or them to bear up and so entangle them, and drive them foul of one another to their utter confusion.

Hodges, *Select Naval Documents*, p. 26

SOURCE 236 Instructions given to the Spanish Commander of the Armada in April 1588 make it clear that English gunnery was superior

Above all, it must be borne in mind that the enemy's object will be to fight at long distance, in consequence of his advantage in artillery, and the large number of artificial fires with which he will be furnished . . . the enemy employs his artillery in order to deliver his fire low and sink his opponent's ships . . .

Hume, *State Papers, Spanish*, Vol. IV, p. 247

SOURCE 237 Drake gives his views on strategy to the Privy Council in March 1588

. . . I think it good that these forces here [in Plymouth] shall be made as strong as . . . convenient, and that for two special causes:—

First, for that they are like to strike the first blow; and secondly, it will put great and good hearts into her Majesty's loving subjects . . . not to fear any invasion in her own country, but to seek God's enemies and her Majesty's where they may be found . . .

Hodges, *Select Naval Documents*, p. 14

SOURCE 238 **Drake reports the victory to Walsingham in July 1588**

God hath given us so good a day in forcing the enemy so far to leeward as I hope in God the Prince of Parma and the Duke of Sidonia shall not shake hands these few days; and whensoever they shall meet, I believe neither of them will greatly rejoice of this day's service . . . I assure your Honour this day's service hath much appalled the enemy, and no doubt but encouraged our army.

From aboard her Majesty's good ship the Revenge, this 29th of July, 1588.

Hodges, *Select Naval Documents*, pp. 28-9

SOURCE 239 The Venetian Ambassador in Rome reports to the Doge about the English victory over the Spanish Armada

" The Queen of England", [the Pope] remarked, "hath no need of the Turk to her help. Have you heard how Drake with his fleet offered battle to the Armada? With what courage! do you think he showed any fear? He is a great captain . . ."

Brown, *State Papers, Venetian*, Vol. VIII, pp. 383-4

SOURCE 240 John Hawkins gives Walsingham an account of the fighting

We met with this fleet somewhat to the westward of Plymouth upon Sunday in the morning being the 21st of July, where we had some small fight with them in the afternoon. By the coming aboard one of the other of the Spaniards, a great ship, a Biscayan, spent her foremast and bowsprit; which was left by the fleet in the sea, and so taken up by Sir Francis Drake the next morning . . .

The Tuesday following, athwart of Portland, we had a sharp and long fight with them, wherein we spent a great part of our powder and shot, so as it was not thought good to deal with them any more till that was relieved.

Monday, the 29th of July, we followed the Spaniards; and all that day had with them a long and great fight, wherein there was great valour showed generally of our company . . . the wind began to blow westerly, a fresh gale, and the Spaniards put themselves somewhat to the northward, where we follow and keep company with them.

E. Hallam Moorhouse (ed.), *Letters of the English Seamen 1587-1808*, Chapman & Hall, 1910, pp. 39-40

TOP: An Elizabethan ship, 1577, a drawing from Holinshed's chronicles
ABOVE: The depot of the Hanseatic League in London

On the map:

ICELAND **FISH**

Atlantic Ocean

White Sea • Archangel

FLAX, HEMP, TIMBER, WAX, TALLOW

TIMBER

COPPER, IRON, TAR, POTASH

NORWAY

SWEDEN

RUSSIA

English exports to Russia and Baltic: **CLOTH, TIN, HERRING**

• Narva

North Sea

Newcastle

Hull

DENMARK

Lübeck

Baltic Sea

• Riga

• Moscow

MUSCOVY

CORN

English exports to Mediterranean: **CLOTH, TIMBER, HERRING, TIN, IRONMONGERY**

Yarmouth
London

Amsterdam
Antwerp

FLANDERS

Hamburg

Danzig

Elbing

GERMANY

Before 1575, **CLOTH** went overland via Amsterdam

FRANCE

Venice

PORTUGAL

Marseilles

Genoa

ITALY

TURKISH

Black Sea

Lisbon

Madrid

SPAIN

Cadiz

EMPIRE

Constantinople

B A R B A R Y

Algiers

Messina

Tunis

Smyrna

Scanderoon

Aleppo

THE LEVANT

CRETE

Tripoli

Mediterranean Sea

SUGAR, SALTPETRE

SILK, INDIGO, COTTON, CINNAMON, PEPPER, NUTMEGS, CLOVES

• Alexandria

0   km   1000

Trade in the Baltic and Mediterranean during Elizabeth's reign

Trade and treasure

Elizabethan seamen contributed greatly to the wealth of their country. Privateering, or pirating on the high seas, became more profitable during the reign (source 241). Most privateers concentrated on the route from the West Indies and South America and, although Spanish treasure fleets were never captured, individual trading ships were. Their cargoes were not quite as exotic as those of the treasure fleet, but commodities such as leather and sugar were very valuable.

More money was brought into the country by legitimate means. The explorers, pirates and privateers were drawn towards the Atlantic and the New World, but English trading ships were more often seen in the Mediterranean. After the Spanish had defeated the Turks at Lepanto in 1571, the Mediterranean became less dangerous for Christian traders. The English took advantage of this and formed trading companies (source 242). By then their ships were strongly built and well armed to resist pirates. The Levant Company, founded in 1581, traded with the eastern Mediterranean. Currants and dyes for cloth were amongst the goods brought back in exchange for English tin. By 1595 the company had 15 ships and 790 seamen, and some of its merchants became very rich.

Not only did trade with the Mediterranean bring wealth to London, but it

149

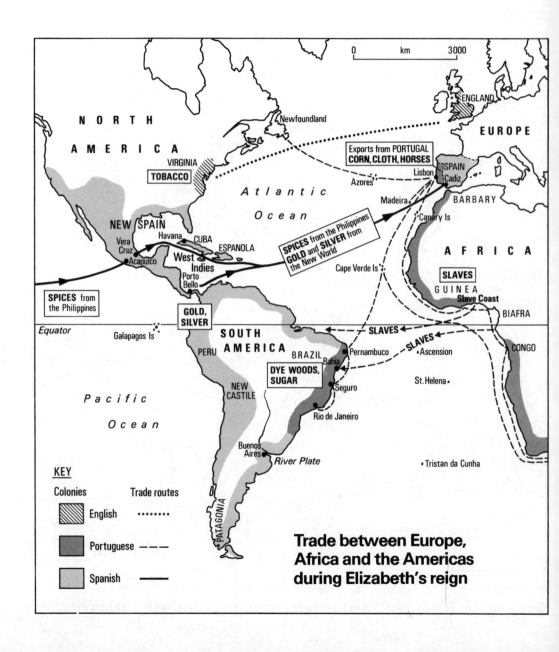

Trade between Europe, Africa and the Americas during Elizabeth's reign

KEY

Colonies

English

Portuguese

Spanish

Trade routes

······

‑ ‑ ‑ ‑

———

Exports from PORTUGAL **CORN, CLOTH, HORSES**

TOBACCO

SPICES from the Philippines **GOLD** and **SILVER** from the New World

SPICES from the Philippines

GOLD, SILVER

DYE WOODS, SUGAR

SLAVES

NORTH AMERICA

EUROPE

ENGLAND

SPAIN
Cadiz

Lisbon

BARBARY

AFRICA

GUINEA
Slave Coast

BIAFRA

CONGO

Newfoundland

VIRGINIA

Atlantic Ocean

Azores

Madeira

Canary Is

Cape Verde Is

NEW SPAIN

Vera Cruz

Acapulco

Havana

CUBA

ESPANOLA

West Indies

Porto Bello

SLAVES

SLAVES

SLAVES

Equator

Galapagos Is

SOUTH AMERICA

PERU

NEW CASTILE

BRAZIL

Bahia

Pernambuco

Seguro

Rio de Janeiro

Ascension

St. Helena

Pacific Ocean

Buenos Aires

River Plate

Tristan da Cunha

PATAGONIA

0   km   3000

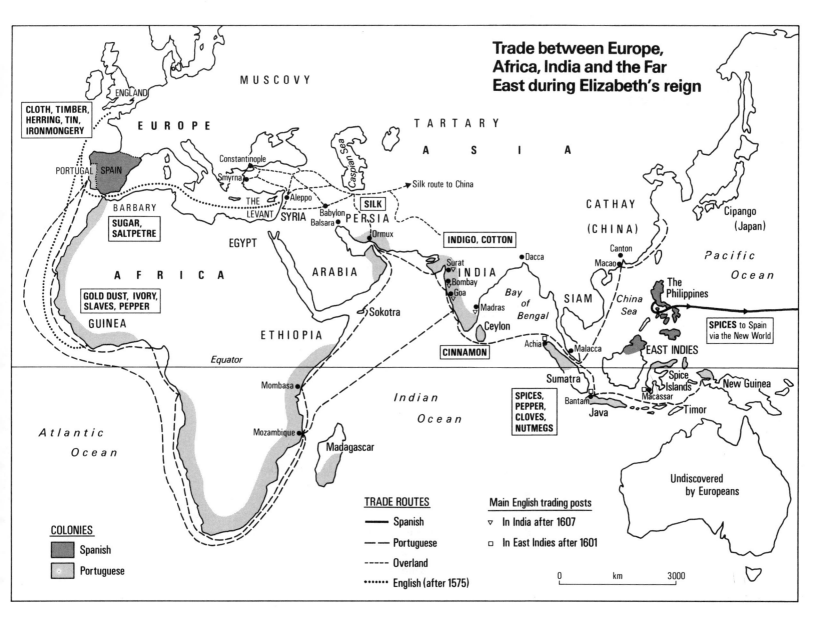

Trade between Europe, Africa, India and the Far East during Elizabeth's reign

CLOTH, TIMBER, HERRING, TIN, IRONMONGERY

ENGLAND

EUROPE

MUSCOVY

TARTARY

ASIA

PORTUGAL SPAIN

BARBARY

SUGAR, SALTPETRE

Constantinople

Smyrna

THE LEVANT

SYRIA

Aleppo

Babylon

Balsara

SILK

PERSIA

Ormux

Caspian Sea

Silk route to China

CATHAY (CHINA)

Cipango (Japan)

EGYPT

AFRICA

ARABIA

INDIGO, COTTON

Surat

Bombay

Goa

INDIA

Dacca

Canton

Macao

Pacific Ocean

GOLD DUST, IVORY, SLAVES, PEPPER

GUINEA

ETHIOPIA

Sokotra

Madras

Bay of Bengal

Ceylon

SIAM

China Sea

The Philippines

SPICES to Spain via the New World

Equator

CINNAMON

Achia

Malacca

EAST INDIES

Mombasa

Indian Ocean

Sumatra

Bantam

Java

Macassar

Spice Islands

New Guinea

Timor

SPICES, PEPPER, CLOVES, NUTMEGS

Atlantic Ocean

Mozambique

Madagascar

COLONIES

Spanish

Portuguese

TRADE ROUTES

——— Spanish

– – – Portuguese

- - - Overland

······· English (after 1575)

Main English trading posts

▽ In India after 1607

▢ In East Indies after 1601

Undiscovered by Europeans

0   km   3000

ABOVE: Sir Walter Raleigh attacks a
port in Trinidad, 1595

inspired traders to go further afield in
search of spices and other far eastern
products. The trade with the East Indies
was something which would bring wealth
to England after Elizabeth's death (source
243). But that later prosperity was made
possible by the sailors and traders of her
reign.

SOURCE 241 English sailors ventured on voyages of discovery and piracy

Of late my countrymen have found out I wot not what voyage into the West Indies,
from whence they have brought some gold, whereby our country is enriched; but of
all that ever adventured into those parts, none have sped better than Sir Francis Drake,
whose success hath far surpassed even his own expectation. One John Frobisher in like
manner, attempting to seek out a shorter cut by the northerly regions into the peacable
sea and kingdom of Cathay, happened, [in] 1577, upon certain islands by the way,
wherein great plenty of much gold appeared . . .

Harrison, *Description of England*, p. 366

SOURCE 242 English overseas trade spread throughout the world by the end of the sixteenth century

. . . whereas in times past their chief trade was into Spain, Portugal, France, Flanders,
Denmark, Norway, Scotland, and Iceland only, now in these days, as men not con-
tented with these journeys, they have sought out the East and West Indies and made
now and then promising voyages, not only into the Canaries and New Spain, but
likewise into Cathay, Muscovy, Tartary, and the regions thereabout, from whence
they bring home great commodities.

Harrison, *Description of England*, pp. 116-17

SOURCE 243 A description of an ideal merchant

A worthy merchant is the heir of adventure, whose hopes hang much upon wind.
Upon a wooden horse he rides through the world, and in a merry gale makes a path
through the seas. He is a discoverer of countries and a finder out of commodities,
resolute in his attempts and royal in his expenses. He is the life of traffic and the main-
tainer of trade, the sailor's master and the soldier's friend. He is the exercise of the

exchange, the honour of credit, the observation of time and the understanding of thrift. His study is number, his care his accounts, his comfort his conscience, and his wealth his good name . . . By his sea gain he makes his land purchase, and by the knowledge of trade finds the key of treasure . . . He plants the earth with foreign fruits, and knows at home what is good abroad. He is neat in apparel, modest in demeanour, dainty in diet and civil in his carriage. In sum, he is the pillar of a city, the enricher of a country, the furnisher of a court, and the worthy servant of a king.

Nicholas Breton, 'The Good and the Badde', 1616, in Alexander B. Grosart (ed.), *The Works in Verse and Prose of Nicholas Breton*, Vol. II, Edinburgh, 1879, p. 9

BELOW: Sir Walter Raleigh landing in Virginia, 1584

Colonies

No overseas colonies were planted in Elizabeth's reign, but it had been the intention of some of the sixteenth-century sailors to found settlements. The Queen had encouraged such enterprises: she granted a charter to Dee, John Davies and Raleigh to set up a "Fellowship for the Discovery of the North West Passage". She gave another to Raleigh to establish his colony at Roanoke in Virginia. However, the Queen's interest, and that of the explorers, was in mining gold. These ventures failed and such expeditions were expensive to finance so they petered out. It was not until the settlers began to grow tobacco on a large scale in the following reign that colonization became a profitable business.

ABOVE: A drawing of a Virginian Indian Chief, 1585, by John White

The Earl of Essex's rebellion, 1601

The background

The late summer of 1588 was a time of rejoicing in England; the 'invincible' Spanish Armada had been defeated. But it was also a time of personal sorrow for Queen Elizabeth. The favourite of the first half of her reign, Robert Dudley, Earl of Leicester, died in the first week of September.

Elizabeth's relationship with Essex

William Cecil, Lord Burghley, was still her principal adviser and Lord Treasurer, but his relationship with the Queen was completely different from Leicester's. In the last years of his life Leicester had introduced his young stepson, Robert Devereux, Earl of Essex, to the Court. By early 1587, at the age of eighteen, he was already spending much of his time in the Queen's company.

SOURCE 244 Anthony Bagot, Essex's servant, describes their relationship

He told me with his own mouth that he looked to be Master of the Horse within these ten days . . .
When she is abroad, nobody near her but my Lord of Essex, and at night, my Lord is at cards, or one game or another with her, that he cometh not to his own lodging till birds sing in the morning . . .

W. B. Devereux (ed.), *Lives and Letters of the Devereux, Earls of Essex in the Reigns of Elizabeth, James I and Charles I*, Vol. I, London, 1853, p. 185

This may give an exaggerated impression of how close the Queen and her new courtier were. It was certainly another six months before Essex was made Master of the Horse, and his appointment was probably a result of Leicester's pleading for him. But there can be little doubt about the Queen's growing affection for him during the next few years.

There were quarrels, but there were reconciliations too. It seems that Elizabeth did not want Essex to be out of her sight and she had refused permission for him to join in the Portugal expedition in 1589. However, Essex was ambitious to gain military glory as well as fame at Court, and left the country against the Queen's wishes. Her summons arrived too late to reach him before he left and as soon as he returned to Court he regained her favour.

SOURCE 245 Elizabeth's summons reveals her displeasure

Essex, your sudden and undutiful departure from our presence and your place of attendance, you may easily conceive how offensive it is, and ought to be, unto us. Our great favours bestowed on you without deserts, hath drawn you thus to neglect and forget your duty.

Williams, *All the Queen's Men*, p. 214

PAGE 154: A lady, supposedly Elizabeth I, dancing with Robert Dudley, Earl of Leicester

BELOW: Robert Devereux, Earl of Essex, c. 1597

Essex's marriage

Essex risked the Queen's anger again by marrying without her knowledge or consent It was hardly surprising that at the age of twenty-three one of the most handsome and dashing young men at Court should marry. His appeal—his looks and charm, and his ancient family and title obviously made up for his constant lack of money.

Elizabeth had always reacted strongly when her courtiers or maids of honour had married, and to marry without her permission was to risk banishment from Court. In Essex's case there was an even greater chance of a violent reaction. She had already sent two young women away from Court when they had appeared to take a fancy to her favourite. So it was quite predictable that when she heard of Essex's marriage to Frances Sidney, the widow of Sir Philip Sidney and daughter of Sir Francis Walsingham, she should fly into a rage. What is interesting is that her anger lasted only a fortnight. Her favourite returned to Court and Elizabeth was even prepared to receive his wife.

Essex as a leader

In politics

Essex had shown by joining the Portugal expedition that being the Queen's favourite courtier was not enough for him. In 1595 he was made a Privy Councillor and he took his work seriously. He attended all the Council meetings and became very knowledgeable about foreign affairs. Elizabeth was impressed by his knowledge and interest and some ambassadors even began to write directly to him as well as writing officially to Burghley.

Perhaps it was useful to Elizabeth to have someone in the Council who could provide a balance, so that Burghley and his son, Robert Cecil, did not appear to be controlling affairs. Certainly there were others who were impressed by Essex's importance and hoped he would be their patron by supporting them and pressing their claims to office.

Cecil's cousins, Anthony and Francis Bacon, were amongst the first to turn to Essex for support, and in 1593 Essex had worked hard (but unsuccessfully) to try to persuade Elizabeth to appoint Francis Bacon Attorney-General.

In the army

In 1596 Essex was given another chance to gain military glory. He was given joint command (with Lord Howard of Effingham) of an expedition to Cadiz. Because Cadiz had been occupied for a fortnight and a large ransom raised from its inhabitants, Essex returned in triumph. Not everyone regarded the expedition as such a great success, and the Queen was annoyed that the £50 000 she had paid out seemed to have been wasted and more was required to pay the seamen's wages. However, there was some booty, and Elizabeth claimed the ransoms from wealthy prisoners. What succeeded in restoring Essex to her favour was the news that the West Indian fleet had arrived in Spain only two days after the English had left; it might have been captured if Essex's plan of waiting off the coast of Portugal had been followed. Not only was he back

ABOVE: Robert Devereux, Earl of Essex, attributed to M. Gheeraerts the Younger

PAGE 157: The death warrant of the Earl of Essex

in favour with the Queen, but he was a popular hero.

Even the failure of another expedition which he led to the Azores the following year could not totally condemn Essex in Elizabeth's eyes. There was a long separation after his return, when Essex remained at his house in Wanstead, but when he eventually appeared at Court at the end of December, there was a great reconciliation and Elizabeth made him Earl Marshal.

His power increases

Essex appeared to be at the height of his glory and seemed to have no rivals. Yet, at the time of his enormous popularity after his return from Cadiz, his friend Francis Bacon had realised that his position was dangerous as well as dazzling and had written a warning letter to him.

SOURCE 246 Francis Bacon's letter tries to show Essex how his character appears to the Queen and then comments on her likely reaction to him

A man of nature not be ruled: that hath the advantage of my affection, and knoweth it; of an estate not grounded to his greatness: of a popular reputation; of a militar dependence . . . I demand whether there can be a more dangerous image than this represented to any monarch living, much more to a lady, and of her Majesty's apprehension . . . I cannot sufficiently wonder at your Lordship's course . . for her Majesty loveth peace . . .

Lytton Strachey, *Elizabeth and Essex*, Chatto & Windus, 1928, p. 117

He advised Essex to concentrate on the Council, rather than on military affairs, and to do everything he could to convince the Queen of his devotion and obedience to her.

His downfall

If Essex had felt able or inclined to follow Bacon's advice, his story might have been very different. It is unlikely that even Bacon would have foreseen the dreadful scene in the Tower of London less than five years later.

SOURCE 247 A modern description of the execution

Essex appeared in a black cloak and hat with three clergymen beside him. Stepping upon the scaffold, he took off his hat, and bowed to the assembled Lords. He spoke long and earnestly — a studied oration, half speech, half prayer. He confessed his sins, both general and particular. He was young he said — he was in his thirty-fourth year — and he 'had bestowed his youth in wantonness, lust and uncleanness' . . . He prayed for the welfare of the Queen, 'whose death I protest I never meant, not violence to her person' . . . The executioner, kneeling before him, asked for his forgiveness, which he granted . . . He rose and took off his doublet; a scarlet waistcoat, with long scarlet sleeves, was underneath. So — tall, splendid, bare-headed, with his fair hair about his shoulders — he stood before the world for the last time. Then, turning, he bowed low before the block; and, saying that he would be ready when he stretched out his arms, he lay down flat upon the scaffold. 'Lord, be merciful to thy prostrate servant!' he cried out, and put his head sideways upon the low block. 'Lord, into thy hands I recommend my spirit.' There was a pause; and all at once the red arms were seen to be extended. The headsman whirled up the axe, and crashed it downwards . . . The man stopped, and, taking the head by the hair, held it up before the onlookers, shouting as he did so, 'God save the Queen!'

Strachey, *Elizabeth and Essex*, pp. 261-3

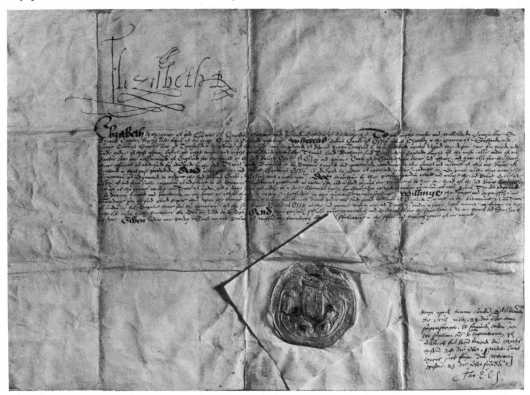

Elizabeth wore a ring he had given her until her death. She had willingly granted his request not be executed in public, but she had been equally clear about signing the death warrant. How was it that this favourite and favoured courtier had been brought to his death, and that the Queen, who felt such affection for him, had had no doubts about the necessity of his death? The immediate answer is that Essex was guilty of treason. He had led a rebellion against the Queen, he had confessed his treason, and the penalty was death. But this only leads us to ask why he rebelled. Look first at the rebellion itself.

The Earl of Essex's rebellion

On the morning of Sunday, 8 February 1601, Essex ignored an order from the Queen to come to Court. She then sent four high officials to his house—the Lord Keeper, the Earl of Worcester, Sir William Knollys, and the Lord Chief Justice. Their servants were forced to stay outside, but they were allowed in, and explained that they were sent from the Queen to find out what the great assembly of people was for. There may have been as many as three hundred people in the courtyard of his house, some of them well known. These included the Earls of Rutland and Southampton, Lord Sandys, Lord Monteagle, Sir Christopher Blount and Sir Charles Danvers.

RIGHT: A contemporary map showing the location of Essex House in London

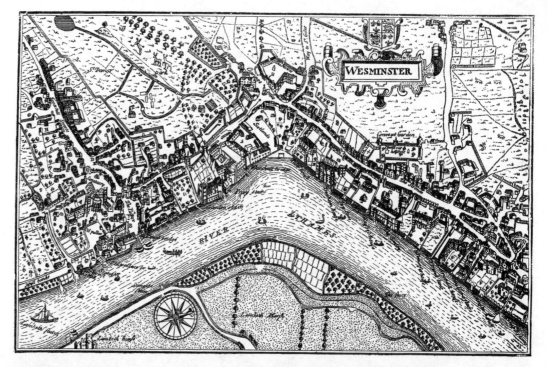

SOURCE 248 Essex deals with the Queen's officials

The Earl of Essex went into the house, and the Lord Keeper etc. followed him, thinking that his purpose had been to speak with them privately, as they had required; and as they were going, some of that disordered company cried "Kill them". And as they were going into the great chamber some cried, "Cast the Great Seal out of the window", some other cried then, "Kill them"; and some other said, "Nay let us shop them up". The Lord Keeper did often call on the Earl of Essex to speak with them privately, thinking still that his meaning had been so, until the Earl brought them into his back chamber, and then gave order to have the further door of that chamber shut fast; and at his going forth out of that chamber, the Lord Keeper pressing again to have spoken with the Earl of Essex, the Earl said, "My Lords, be patient a while, and stay here, and I will go into London and take order with the Mayor and Sheriff for the city, and will be here again within this half-hour"; and so departed from the Lord Keeper etc. leaving the Lord Keeper, etc. and divers of the gentlemen prisoners in that chamber . . .

Devereux, *Lives*, Vol. II, p. 143

His strategy

As Essex and his followers left, there were cries of 'To the Court! To the Court!', but Essex in fact turned towards the City. He was possibly relying on his past popularity there for support, but he was disappointed. Though Essex shouted as he rode through the Sunday crowds 'For the Queen! For the Queen! A plot is laid for my life' no one rushed to join him. Moreover, the vague promise that he had had the night before that Sheriff Smyth would back him with a thousand armed men proved false. When he finally caught Sheriff Smyth slipping out of his own back door, he was told that there were no men and that there had never been any promise to supply them.

Too late Essex now turned back towards the Court. The Privy Council had acted. Thomas, Lord Burghley, the Earl of Cumberland and the Knight Marshal had proclaimed throughout the city that Essex and his followers were traitors, and promised complete pardon to those who deserted him. This caused many to slip

LEFT: Essex House from the Thames, showing a boat mooring at the steps

away unnoticed from Essex's party. He now decided to head back to Essex House. Again, however, the Council had out-manoeuvred him. A chain had been placed across Lud Gate on the city walls to prevent Essex's return that way and when Essex charged it the pikemen there stoutly resisted the onslaught. Essex retreated to the Thames. Here he found some boats and managed to get back to Essex House by the river. His last hope now was to negotiate with the Queen using his prisoners as hostages.

His defeat

Yet again he was to be disappointed. Sir Ferdinando Gorges, who got to Essex House before him, decided to save his own skin. He released Lord Keeper Egerton and the others and went with them to the Palace.

Essex's rebellion was at an end. He hastily burned all his private papers and then went up on to the roof to ask for terms with the Lord Admiral, Howard of Effingham, who by now had cannon and musket trained on Essex House. The Lord Admiral refused to make terms with rebels. For a while Essex thought of fighting it out to the bitter end. Eventually, however, he decided to surrender on three conditions: that they should be treated in a civil way; that they should have a fair trial; and that Mr Ashton, his chaplain, should be allowed to attend him in prison for the good of his soul. The rebellion had lasted just 12 hours.

It is not even clear what Essex intended to do if he was successful. It seems he wanted to capture the person of the Queen (though he wished her no harm) and no doubt he would insist on Court offices for his followers. It is difficult to believe that the rebellion was part of a well-considered plan, and maybe to ask what Essex intended to achieve is to ask a question he could not have answered satisfactorily himself. But what we can try to understand is what drove him and his followers to the demonstration of 8 February.

Why did Essex rebel?

Political developments

What had been happening since Essex's reappearance at Court at the end of 1597? He had continued to press for a great offensive against Spain but the Cecils had opposed him.

There were more new appointments to be made. Once again Essex had his own candidates in mind. On 1 July 1598 during a meeting of the Council, Elizabeth refused Essex's suggestion that Sir George Carew should be the new Lord Deputy in Ireland. In a temper Essex turned his back on the Queen. Infuriated by this Elizabeth stood up and punched Essex on the ear. Essex whirled round and was about to draw his sword when the Earl of Nottingham intervened. Essex stormed out of the chamber and refused to attend Court. He thought himself to be the injured person and not the Queen.

He fled to his house at Wanstead. While he was away Elizabeth was distracted and distressed by the last illness of Burghley, her most trusted councillor for over forty years, who died on 4 August.

Essex could not bear to feel that he had been wronged by the Queen.

SOURCE 249 Essex writes to Elizabeth

Madam, — When I think how I have preferred your beauty above all things, and received no pleasure in life but by the increase of your favour towards me, I wonder at myself what cause there could be to make me absent myself one day from you. But when I remember that your Maj. hath, by the intolerable wrong you have done both me and yourself, not only broken all laws of affection, but done against the honour of your sex, I think all places better than that where I am, and all dangers well undertaken, so I might retire myself from the memory of my false, inconstant, and beguiling pleasures . . . I was never proud, till your Maj. sought to make me too base. And now since my destiny is no better, my despair shall be as my love was, without repentance. I will as a subject and an humble servant owe my life, my fortune, and all that is in me; but this place is not fit for me, for she which governs this world is weary of me, and I of the World. I must commend my faith to be judged by Him who judgeth all hearts, since on earth I find no right. Wishing your Maj. all comforts and joys in the world, and no greater punishment for your wrongs to me, than to know the faith of him you have lost, and the baseness of those you shall keep,

Your Majesty's most humble servant,
R. Essex

Devereux, *Lives*, Vol. I, pp. 493-4

Meanwhile, English forces had suffered a disaster in Ireland. The Earl of Tyrone had attacked and completely defeated the English army which was marching to relieve a fort on the Blackwater. The whole of northern Ireland, as far south as Dublin, seemed open to the rebels. As soon as Essex heard this news, he wrote another letter to Elizabeth, offering his services, and hurried to Whitehall. Elizabeth, however, would not see him, and the Lord Keeper Egerton explained to him how dangerous his position was and how he must beg the Queen's forgiveness. Essex's reply to Egerton reveals his attitude.

SOURCE 250 Essex writes to Lord Keeper Egerton to explain why he will not attend Court

The indissoluble duty which I owe to Her Majesty is only the duty of allegiance, which I never will, nor never can, fail in. The duty of attendance is no indissoluble duty. I owe to her Majesty the duty of an Earl and Lord Marshal of England. I have been content to do Her Majesty the service of a clerk, but can never serve her as a villain or slave . . . But, say you, I must yield and submit; I can neither yield myself to be guilty or this imputation laid upon me to be just. I owe so much to the author of all truth, as I can never yield falsehood to be truth, nor truth falsehood . . . I patiently bear all, and sensibly feel all, that I then received when this scandal was given me. Nay more, when the vilest of all indignities are done unto me, doth religion enforce me to sue? Doth God require it? Is it impiety not to do it? What, cannot princes, err? Cannot subjects receive wrong? Is an earthly power or authority infinite? Pardon me, pardon me, my good Lord, I can never subscribe to these principles. Let Solomon's fool laugh when he is stricken; let those that mean to make their profit of princes shew to have no sense of prince's injuries; let them acknowledge an infinite absoluteness on earth, that do not believe in an absolute infiniteness in heaven. As for me, I have received wrong and feel it. My cause is good, I know it; and whatsoever come, all the powers on earth can never shew more strength and constancy in oppressing, than I can shew in suffering whatsoever can or shall be imposed on me.

Essex

Devereux, *Lives*, Vol, I, pp. 501-2

ABOVE: Robert Devereux, Earl of Essex

PAGE 160: Elizabeth I at Wanstead House

Changes in Essex's relationship with the Queen

It did not seem that Essex was in any mood to apologise and beg the Queen's forgiveness. However, he did return to Court. We do not know when, why, or how he was received, but he was taking an active part in Council debates on Ireland in the winter of 1598-9, and we know that he danced with Elizabeth at the Twelfth Night celebrations in January, 1599.

Soon afterwards Sir Richard Bingham, the most experienced Irish commander, died and the question of whom to send as Lord Deputy to Ireland became urgent. Essex argued that it should be 'some prime man of nobility, strong in power, honour and wealth, in favour with military men, who had been before general of an army'. Few men had all these qualifications, and few wanted the position. In March 1599 Essex himself was appointed. Just before this Elizabeth had become extremely angry when she found a book by John Hayward, *A History of Henry IV*, dedicated to the Earl of Essex. She seemed to feel that the link between Essex and Henry Bolingbroke, whose deposition of King Richard II was described in the book, was unmistakable. The author could not be convicted for treason, but he spent the rest of the Queen's reign in the Tower of London.

Essex in Ireland

Essex arrived in Ireland in April 1599 and immediately his behaviour provoked disputes with Elizabeth. He appointed one of his circle of friends, the Earl of Southampton, as commander of the cavalry. Elizabeth disliked Southampton and had forbidden Essex to give him any particular office.

SOURCE 251 Elizabeth's angry letter to her Lord Deputy

We not only not allowed of your desire for him, but did expressly forbid it, and being such a one whose counsel can be of little, and experience of less, use . . . It is therefore strange to us, knowing his worth by your report . . . will dare thus to value your own pleasing in things unnecessary, and think by your own private arguments to carry for your own glory a matter wherein our pleasure to the contrary is made notorious.

E. G. Atkinson (ed.), *Calendar of State Papers, Ireland, 1599-1600*, HMSO, 1899, pp. 100-01

Another source of irritation, both to the Queen and to the rest of the Council, was the way in which Essex created knights. During the unsuccessful siege of Rouen in 1591 he had made twenty-one knights. Then on the Cadiz expedition of 1596, together with Lord Howard of Effingham, he had made sixty-eight. Aware of the Queen's extreme displeasure at this, he created about eighty knights during the five months he was in Ireland.

SOURCE 252 A report from John Chamberlain, dated 23 August 1599

It is much marvelled that this humour should so possess him that not content with his first dozens and scores, he should thus fall to huddle them up by halfe hundreds; and it is noted as a strange thing that a subject in the space of seven or eight years . . . should upon so little service and small desert make more knights than are in all the realm besides, and it is doubted that if he continue this course he will shortly bring in tag and rag, cut and long tayle, and so draw the order into contempt.

L. Stone, *The Crisis of the Aristocracy 1558–1641*, O.U.P., 1965, p. 73

What really infuriated the Queen was Essex's failure as a military commander. Tyrone, the rebel leader, controlled Ulster, and the Queen's orders had been to attack him there. However, Essex remained further south in Leinster and Munster, and spent his time taking unimportant castles. His army dwindled and Essex blamed other officers for the men's desertion.

SOURCE 253 Essex writes to Elizabeth explaining the loss of manpower

Your army, which never yet abandoned the body of any principal commander being dead, doth now run away from their chief commander, being alone and in flight [he meant Clifford] . . . your people had rather be hanged for cowardice, than killed or hurt in service.

J. B. Black, *The Reign of Elizabeth*, O.U.P., 1936, p. 19

BELOW: Lord Burghley with his son, Robert Cecil

Elizabeth makes new appointments

While things were going badly in Ireland, Essex received upsetting news from England; in May 1599 Robert Cecil was given the Mastership of the Court of Wards Essex particularly wanted the position which made the holder the guardian of the estates of all young nobles who inherited lands before the age of twenty-one. There was huge profit to be made from such a position. Essex discovered that Burghley who had held the office till his death in 1598, made a good income from the office. For example, official receipts on nine wardships which Burghley handled totalled £906.3s.4d, but in addition secret payments had been made to a total of £3016.13s.4d. (Figures from J. Hurstfield, *The Queen's Wards. Wardships and Marriages under Elizabeth I* Longmans, 1958, p. 343)

In July 1596 Cecil had been appointed Secretary, and in October 1597 he became Chancellor of the Duchy of Lancaster. This latest appointment seemed to mark his complete emergence as his father's successor and a successful political rival to Essex himself.

Essex was thinking of returning with his army to England, but the Queen wrote forbidding him to come until he had fought in the north. At the end of August he moved into Ulster, but no battle took place. Instead, Essex and Tyrone met and a truce was arranged, but the rebels gave up none of their land or forts. When the news reached her, Elizabeth wrote saying she thought the truce was useless, and Essex must subdue the rebels. However, before the letter reached him, Essex had decided to leave Ireland and seek an interview with the Queen.

Essex's return

On 28 September Essex arrived at Court.

SOURCE 254 Rowland Whyte, a friend of the Sidney family, witnessed Essex's arrival and described Elizabeth's reactions

On Michaelmas eve, about ten o'clock in the morning, my Lord of Essex lighted at court gate in post, and made all haste up to the presence, and so to the privy chamber, and staid not till he came to the Queen's bed-chamber, where he found the Queen newly up, her hair about her face; he kneeled unto her, kissed her hands, and had some private speech with her, which seemed to give him great contentment; for, coming from Her Majesty to go shift himself in his chamber, he was very pleasant, and thanked God, though he had suffered much trouble and storms abroad, he found a sweet calm at home.

'Tis much wondered at here that he went so boldly to her Majesty's presence, she not being ready, and he so full of dirt and mire that his very face was full of it. About eleven he was ready, and went up again to the Queen and conferred with her till half an hour after twelve. As yet all was well, and her usage very gracious towards him.

[After dinner] . . . he went up to the Queen but found her much changed in that small time, for she began to call him in question for his return, and was not satisfied in the manner of his coming away, and leaving all things at so great hazard. She appointed the Lords to hear him, and so they went to Council in the afternoon; Lord Chamberlain, Lord North, Mr. Secretary and Mr. Comptroller; and he went with them, where they sat an hour. But nothing was determined, or yet known. Belike it is referred to a full council, for all the Lords are sent for to be here this day. It is mistrusted that, for his disobedience, he shall be committed; but that will be seen either this day or tomorrow.

Devereux, *Lives*, Vol. II, pp. 77-9

The next day Essex was examined by the Privy Council on the following six charges:
That he had written presumptuous letters from Ireland.
That in Ireland he had acted contrary to his instructions.
That his departure from Ireland had been rash and irresponsible.
That he had been overbold in breaking into Her Majesty's bed-chamber.
That he had created too many idle knights.
That he had contemptuously disobeyed Her Majesty's instructions by returning to England.

Two days later on Monday, 1 October 1599, Elizabeth ordered Essex to be confined at York House in the custody of the Lord Keeper. Essex was ill at this time and his illness seemed to enhance his popularity. There were rumours that he was dying, and also that he was plotting with King James VI of Scotland to overthrow Elizabeth. Pamphlets were written defending him and attacking his enemies.

Essex is banned from Court

On 5 June 1600 a full enquiry was held into Essex's doings and finally on 26 August 1600 the Queen made her wishes known. Essex was to be free to go home but he could never come to Court again.

Essex's freedom left him without any power. Moreover, he was now in serious financial trouble. Essex's chief single source of money was the farm of sweet wines, which he had been given in 1590 for ten years.

The farm was a grant from the Queen for the holder to collect customs duties on sweet wines from the Mediterranean countries. Essex let someone else organize the collection of the customs, but after paying him and a fixed amount to the Crown, the rest, about £2 000 a year, went into Essex's own pocket. The grant of this farm ran out on Michaelmas Day (29 September) 1600.

His financial difficulties

By 1600 Essex's lavish style of living, his collection of a huge following of retainers, and his expenditure on military expeditions-particularly the Irish expedition of 1599-had put him into debt. He was living now on credit from London bankers, he owed £15 000 to individuals, apart from a large debt to the Queen, and his landed estate brought in about £3 000 a year. He desperately needed the farm of sweet wines to keep his creditors at bay.

SOURCE 255 Essex's desperate letter to Elizabeth begging for money

If conscience did not tell me, that, without imploring your Majesty's goodness at this time, most dear and most admired Sovereign, I should not only lose the present support of my poor estate, but the hope of any ability to do your Majesty future service, and not that alone, but the means of satisfying a great number of hungry and annoying creditors, which suffer me in my retired life to have no rest; I would appear still before your Majesty as a mute person. But since this day se'night, the lease which I hold by your Majesty's beneficence expireth, and that farm is both my chiefest maintenance and mine only means of compounding with the merchants to whom I am indebted . . . If my creditors will take for payment many ounces of my blood, or the taking away of

this farm would only for want finish my body, your Majesty should never hear of this suit. For in myself I find no boldness to importune, and from myself I can draw no argument to solicit. The only suit which I can make willingly, and must make continually unto your Majesty is, that you will once again look with gracious eyes upon your Majesty's humblest, faithfullest, and more than most devoted vassal,

22nd Sept. 1600   *Essex*

Devereux, *Lives*, Vol. II, pp. 125-6

SOURCE 256 Essex's letter to Elizabeth pleading for an end to his exile in the country

If I should as often present your Majesty, most dear and most admired Sovereign, with mine humble lines, as mine oppressed spirit would disburthen itself, I should be presumptious and importunate; if I should as seldom write as your Maj. gives me encouragement, I should be dumb and desperate and I am confident that your Maj. inseparable justice in both kinds pleadeth for me. When you say, Why is Essex silent? your Maj. answers yourself, His infinitely affectionate heart is overawed with duty. When your Maj. saith, How dare he write now? you likewise answer, His present fear is overcome by passion, By passion I say, tyrannous to me, but reverent to your Maj. Out of that passion my soul cries out unto your Maj. for grace, for access, and for an end of this exile. If your Maj. grant this suit, you are most gracious, whatsoever else you deny or take away. If this cannot be obtained, I must doubt whether that the means to preserve life, and the granted liberty, have been favours or punishments; for till I may appear in your gracious presence, and kiss your Majesty's fair correcting hand, time itself is a perpetual night, and the whole world but a sepulchre unto your Majesty's humblest vassal,

18th Oct. 1600. *Essex*

Devereux, *Lives*, Vol. II, p. 127

LEFT: Elizabeth I, an allegorical portrait 'Time and Death', painted after her death

Elizabeth had made no decision on the farm of sweet wines. Then at the end of October she announced that she would not renew the farm, but would administer the customs herself.

Rumours of rebellion

Plots and rumours then began. There was some correspondence with James VI of Scotland. It was said by Essex's followers that Robert Cecil was a friend of the Spaniards, and that Sir Walter Raleigh wanted to kill Essex.

In the new year of 1601 plans were being made for taking over Whitehall Palace. But Essex's list of those who would support him was inaccurate and extremely optimistic.

Some of Essex's supporters persuaded the Lord Chamberlain's men to put on a special performance of Shakespeare's *Richard II* at the Globe on Saturday, 7 February. For the first time the abdication scene was included, and Elizabeth was furious. She summoned Essex to attend the Council, but he refused to leave his house, saying that he feared for his life. Next morning the rebellion began.

Solving the problem

Why did Essex rebel?

Can you now answer the question. Consider Essex's ambitions and look at two contemporary assessments of his motives and character (sources 257, 258).

SOURCE 257 The French Ambassador's view of Essex

He is a man who in nowise contents himself with a petty fortune and aspires to greatness . . .

Andrew Herault Maisse, *Journal 1597*, G. B. Harrison & R. A. Jones (trans.), London, 1931, p. 116

SOURCE 258 An English courtier's opinion of Essex

It resteth with me in my opinion that ambition thwarted in its career doth speedily lead on to madness. His speeches of the Queen becometh no man who had mens sana [a sound mind (in a sound body)].

Harington, *Nugae Antiquae*, p. 179

1. In what ways had Essex's desires been thwarted?
2. Do you think there were any weaknesses in Essex's nature which conflicted with his ambitions?
3. What changes had occurred in Elizabeth's feelings for Essex and in the relationship between them?

4. Read Sir Robert Cecil's account of Essex's confession (source 259). Do you think this throws any light on Essex's motives?

SOURCE 259 Sir Robert Cecil's account of Essex's confession about the rebellion written on 4 March 1601

Sir George Carew,

I hope it shall not seem to you any neglect that you have heard no more from me these 21 days and more considering how great and important causes have held not only her Majesty but all her Council ... from all other business of any other place but here at home, where no small blow was like to be struck ... if God had not in his providence hindered their designs. You shall therefore understand that the 19 February the Earl was arraigned in Westminster Hall before 25 peers ... At the bar the Earl laboured to extenuate his fault by denying that he ever meant any harm to her Majesty's person, and by pretending that he took arms principally to save himself from my Lord Cobham and Sir Walter Raleigh who he gave out should have murdered him in his house on Saturday night. He pretended also an intention he had to remove one, with some others, from the Queen, as one who would sell the Kingdom of England to the Infanta of Spain ... but when he saw himself condemned, and found

that Sir John Davies, Sir Ferdinando Gorges and Sir Charles Danvers and Sir Christopher Blount, had confessed all the conferences that were held at Drury House by his directions for the surprising of the Queen and the Tower, which argued a premeditated treason (while he laboured to have had it prove only a sudden putting himself into strength and flying into the city for fear of being committed over night when the lords sent for him, which upon my faith to you (to whom I will not lie) was only to have reproved him for his unlawful assemblies, and to have wished him to leave the City and retire into the Country) he then broke out ... in these words: that his confederates, who now had accused him, had been principal inciters of him, and not he of them to work his access to the Queen with force. After he had been in the Tower one night he sent ... to move her Majesty to send unto him the Lord Keeper, Lord Treasurer, Lord Admiral, and me, the Secretary, that he might now ... confess ... When it pleased Her Majesty the next day to send us four unto him ... he did with very great penitency (as ever I saw) confess how sorry he was that he made so obstinate denials at the bar, desiring that he might set down in writing his whole Project ... which he hath done in four sheets of paper ... declaring first, that he sent divers articles to be considered of ... whether it were not

good at the same time of coming to Court to possess the Tower ... Next, that Sir Christopher Blount should take the Court gate, Sir John Davies should with some company command the Hall, and go up into the great Chamber ... and to have seized on the Halbards of the Guard, which you know stand piled up against the wall. And Sir Charles Danvers should have ... made good that place whereby my Lord of Essex with the Earls of Southampton, Rutland and some other noblemen should have gone into the Queen, and then having her in their possession, to have used the shadow of her authority for changing the government; and so to have called a parliament and have condemned all these that should have been scandalised to have misgoverned that state.

This is the substance of his confession ... then he did most passionately desire ... forgiveness at the hands of those persons whom he had particularly called his Enemies; protesting that when he first resolved of this Rebellious Act he saw not what better pretext he could have than a particular quarrel ... then being earnestly urged still to say what he knew ... of that injurious imputation to me ... he did freely aquit me from any such matter, and was ashamed to have spoken it ... and professed withall to bear no malice to those others, the Lord Cobham and Sir Walter Raleigh, whom he had named his enemies, and by whom he knew no other than that they were true servants to the Queen and the State.

After that he made a very humble suit to the Queen that he might have the favour to die privately in the Tower, which Her Majesty granted, and for which he gave most humble thanks. The 25 of February, he suffered in the Tower, with very great patience and humility . . . for . . . no man living could die more Christianly than he did.

Letters from Sir Robert Cecil to Sir George Carew.
Camden Society, 1864, Vol. 88, pp. 67-72

RIGHT: Henry Wriothesley, 3rd Earl of Southampton, by John de Critz

ABOVE: The Gunpowder Plot

Why did others join the rebellion?

Essex would never have been able to rebel if he had not had some support.

There is no easy answer. The one thing which virtually all his followers had in common was that they were penniless. All of the aristocrats who joined Essex—the Earls of Southampton, Rutland, Sussex and Bedford, and Lords Mounteagle, Cromwell and Sandys—were short of money.

Financial crises

They all spent extravagantly—Rutland for example between 1597 and 1601 spent £12 400 on pleasure.

Many had to provide for relatives. It was a rule in common law that widows were entitled to a third of any estate money left by their husbands. Six of the conspirators had had to pay out in previous years for widows. Essex's mother was still alive in 1601 and his step great-grand-mother had only died in 1600.

Bedford's step-grandmother and aunt were alive; Rutland had a step-grand-mother and aunt alive; Mounteagle's step-grandmother was still alive; and Sandys's mother had outlived her husband for forty years and had only just died.

All were heavily in debt, and trying to raise cash by land sales (source 260).

SOURCE 260 The debts of the conspirators in 1601, all figures are to the nearest £1 000

	Land sales 1591–1600	Date	Private Debts	Total sales and debt
2nd Earl of Essex	£40 000	1601	£25 000	£65 000
5th Earl of Rutland		1601	£5 000	£5 000
3rd Earl of Southampton	£20 000	1601	£8 000	£28 000
5th Earl of Sussex	£20 000	1601	?	£20 000
3rd Earl of Bedford	£1 000	1601	£7 000	£8 000
3rd Lord Sandys	£1 000	1601	£3 000	£4 000
3rd Lord Cromwell	£10 000	1601		£10 000

Stone, *Crisis of the Aristocracy*, p. 778

Similarly most of the other rebels had financial motives. There were unemployed captains such as Thomas Lee, William Green and John Selby, and knights such as Sir William Constable, Sir Thomas West and Sir Ferdinando Gorges, who were heavily in debt.

Religious toleration

Sir Christopher Blount said afterwards that Essex had promised 'a toleration of religion'. Sir Christopher Blount himself, and Sir Charles Danvers, were Catholics. Many who fought for Essex were later in the Catholic Gunpowder Plot of 5 November 1605, such as Robert Catesby Francis Tresham, John Wright, Christopher Wright John Grant, Robert Winter and Sir Edward Beynlam.

But Essex's cause attracted a number of Puritans. He allowed them to preach in the courtyard of Essex House and this gave the impression that trouble might be brewing there.

Political power and status

Some, like Sir William Constable, Sir Edward Littleton, Sir George Devereux, Sir Robert Cross and Sir Griffin Markham, were unsuccessful courtiers. Like Essex, they had not been given positions for which they had hoped. Possibly they hoped he would be able to give them court offices when he had succeeded in wresting power from Elizabeth.

Glossary

abdication   act of giving up the throne
abidings   homes, dwellings
abroad   out and about
abrogated   abolished, annulled
abundant   excessive, large scale
accession   coming into possession of the throne
accoutred   dressed
admonish   charge or order
adversaries   enemies, opponents
affright   cause terror
allow of   acknowledge, permit
allegiance   the duties and ties of a subject to his sovereign
amity   friendship
Anti-Christ   the title of a great personal opponent of Christ
apparel   clothing
appertain   relate, belong to
apprehended   captured, caught
arable land   land used for growing crops
ardent   eager, enthusiastic
arquebuse   long-barrelled musket or gun
arraign   put on trial
artifice   ingenious devices or tricks
artificiers   craftsmen
artillery   large guns
ascertain   find out
assize   measurement
athwart   across from
auditors   listeners
aught   anything
augmented   added to, supplemented
auguries   omens
authority spiritual   power or right to enforce obedience in religious matters
ballast   any heavy material, placed in a ship's hold to sink her to such a depth as to prevent her from capsizing whilst in motion

banished   expelled, sent away
barren   dull, unresponsive
base   humble, worthless
baseless   worthlessness
bawdry   vulgarity, obscenity
bawdy   obscene
bearwards   wardens or keepers of bears
Bedlam   Hospital of St. Mary of Bethlehem, for the insane
beggared   made inadequate
beguiling   distracting, diverting
beneficence   kind gift, donation
benevolence   generosity
biographer   writer of someone's life story
bill   a weapon carried by soldiers and watchmen, a blade with a long wooden handle
booty   plunder, profit
bowsprit   a wooden spar projecting from the upper end of the bow of a sailing ship
brazier   a dish or tray for holding burning charcoal
broil   quarrel, disturbance
bruit   rumour
Bull   formal document issued by the Pope
bulwarks   fortifications
burgesses   magistrates or members of the governing body of the town
bussing   to kiss but in a promiscuous sense (Robert Herrick, "We busse our wantons, but our wives we kisse")
cadets   younger sons
cassock   long loose coat or gown
catalyst   someone or something who helps to bring about change; here: a centre of reaction or opposition
Cathay   China
caul   a netted cap worn by women, a net for the hair
censurers   critics, commentators

charges   formal accusations
chattels   property, goods
civil in his carriage   orderly, decent
cleaver   a butcher's chopper for cutting up carcasses
clipping   embracing
cocksure   secure, safe
comely   pleasant, agreeable
commissioner   the royal representative
commodities   goods, merchandise, produce
compassed   contrived
compassing   encircling
compounding with   settling a debt with, paying up
concernment   interest, importance
coney-catcher   cheat, swindler
confederates   friends, allies
confer   grant, give
conformity   compliance with accepted beliefs
constancy   faithfulness, perseverance, firmness
contemporary   belonging to the same age or period
contrivances   plots
cornering of corn   buying up the whole available supply of corn so that it can be sold later at a higher price
corporal punishment   physical punishments
councillor   member of group of advisers
countenance   appearance
counterfeited   falsified, disguised
counterfeit licences   forged or faked permissions
cozeners   cheats, frauds
culling   cuddling
curate   clergyman's assistant, also a priest
damask   rich, woven silk fabric
deemed   judged, considered, thought
demeanour   conduct, behaviour
demembering   cutting off a limb

demi-paradise   semi-paradise
designs   plans
disburthen   unburden
disposition   control, arrangement
dissenter   person who disagreed with the doctrine of the Church of England
dissolution   dismissal of parliament
dissolution of the monasteries   the breakup of the monasteries brought about by Henry VIII during his reformation of the Church in England
divers   various
diverse   varied, several
doctrine   belief, something which is laid down as true
dominions   lands subject to a particular ruler or king, kingdom, realm
durst   dared
edict   an order issued by a monarch or someone in authority
Egyptian   gypsy
eke   also, too
emporium   an important centre of commerce and trade
endeavours   attempts, efforts
enforce   compel observance
engender   produce, develop,
engines of state   high level executives, ministers or advisers
enmity   hostility, bad feeling
evinces   shows, indicates
esquires   gentlemen ranked belov knights
execution   carrying out
exhorts   begs, urges
expediency   political consideration, advantage
expireth   lapses, ends
extenuate   to lessen, reduce
factions   associations, groups
faculty   ability, aptitude
fain   ready, eager
falchion   sword
felon   thief

felony   theft
fences   professional swordsmen who fenced in public shows
fervency   eagerness, ardour
feudal households   households and supporters of the great lords
feuds   hostilities, serious quarrels and disagreements
flagrant   obvious and offensive, glaring
flax   linen cloth made from fibres of the flax plant
fleering   to laugh coarsely, gibe, jeer
fond   foolish
forbear   avoid, shun, abstain
foremast   mast nearest the bow of a ship
fortitude   strength and courage
frigate   a light and swift sailing ship
gad   wander about idly, with no purpose
galleon   a large warship
game resistance   a spirited fight
gentles   people
gentry   the class below the nobility
groundlings   the people who watched plays from the pit of the theatre
habit   clothes
habitations   dwellings, homes
harbouring   sheltering, hiding
harquebussiers   soldiers armed with arquebuses (or early types of muskets, guns)
headborough   parish constable
heathen idolatry   pagan or non-Christian worship
hemp   a plant used to make strong cloth
heretic   a Christian, usually Roman Catholic, who rejected the teachings of the Roman Catholic Church
high commission   the highest authority
hiring-fairs   a market or fair where servants are hired

houses of bawdry   brothels, houses of ill-repute, even inns and taverns
human agency   human help
humour   mood, state of mind
impiety   ungodliness
impolitic   unwise
importune   to ask urgently, urge
importunate   troublesome
impotent   people unfit to work
imputation   accusation, charge
incapacitated   unfit, unable
inconstant   frequently changing, variable
incontinency   lacking in self-control
incorrigible   beyond correction or reform
indenture   contract
indifferent   neutral, impartial
indignities   insults
indissoluble   everlasting, never-ending, unbreakable
Infanta   a daughter of the King and Queen of Spain
infinite   endless
innovators   revolutionaries, holders of new ideas
insinuate   introduce by devious methods
instrument   a person sent to perform a task by someone else; the means of (doing something)
interludes   dramatic and short plays, usually humourous
invincible   unconquerable
Jesuits   Roman Catholic priests belonging to the Society of Jesus
jubilee   special time of rejoicing declared by the Pope
jurisdiction   range or area of power and law
just commendation   deserved approval
lamentations   cries of grief

lateen yard   rope from which a triangular sail—the lateen sail—is suspended about 45° to the mast

leger   representative agent

lewd   obscene, vulgar

liturgy   the form of Church service (*The Book of Common Prayer*)

Lutheran   German Protestant followers of Martin Luther

malignant heretic   dangerous follower of a different religion

mandates   legal commands, orders

manifest   (to make) plain, obvious, proven, shown

Marchioness   the wife or widow of a Marquis

mark   coin, equivalent of 8 oz. in gold or silver

Massing priest   a priest who performs Roman Catholic Mass

matriarch   a female head of an organisation or family; the Queen

mechanical contrivance   a stage prop moved by mechanical power

meslynne   mixed grain; rye mixed with wheat

metre   poetic rhythm

Michaelmas   September 29th, festival of St. Michael

minion   idol

misdemeanours   offences against the law, crimes

mizen   a sail set on the mast at the stern of a ship

morals   morality plays

mortality   loss of life

much ado   fuss

Muscovy   Russia

mute   silent, quiet

niche   a position suited to the merits of the person

oppressive   unjustly harsh

oration   delivery of a speech

Orcades   Orkney Isles

Our Lady   Lady Day, March 25th

Our pleasure   the royal will

pageant   richly costumed parade

palmistry   practice of telling a person's character by inspection of the palm of the hand

papists   Roman Catholics, believing in the Pope's supremacy

passengers   vagabonds

pastorals   poems or plays in which country life is portrayed

patronage   the practice, usually Royal, of giving financial support or encouraging and favouring a person

peerless   unequalled

penitency   sorrow, regret

penitents   repenters

peradventure   possibly, maybe

perchance   by chance

perfidy   treachery, breach of faith

periwig-pated   wig-wearing

perplexities   distress, confusion

pertaining   belonging

pessimism   tendency to expect the worst

physiognomy   foretelling of the future from the features and lines of the face

pillar of a city   strength and support of a city

pinnace   a small ship with oars and sails

plaints   accusations, charges, complaints

planted   founded or established colonies

players   actors

plurality   majority

poll their tops (that . . .)   to behead people (who . . .)

poop   the highest deck of a ship

portents   signs, omens

Portingals   Portuguese

posterity   succeeding generations

potentate   a prince, monarch, ruler

prejudicial   damaging

prelacy   system of church government by bishops

prelate   a church dignitary of high rank i.e. Bishop or Archbishop

premeditated   thought-out beforehand

presumptuous   impertinent, challenging

Prince   sovereign ruler, monarch, Queen

privateering   the use of sailing ships, armed and officered by private persons who are given permission by the government to attack and rob foreign merchant ships

privity   private knowledge and support

proclamation   official and formal public announcement

proctors   people with licences to beg for alms on behalf of lepers and others but prohibited from begging for themselves

procuration   one person representing another on official business

prodigality   reckless extravagance

profanation   show contempt, treat with irreverence

professed   openly declared

(royal) progress   journey of the Queen and court around the country

prorogation   the discontinuing of the meetings of parliament for a time without dissolving it

proscribed   outlawed, denounced, forbidden

prow   front part of a ship

quartered   divided into quarters

quartering   to cut a person into quarters after they have been executed

quelled   suppressed, put down

querns   circular stones for grinding corn

quick the tender or sensitive flesh of any part of the body (e.g. under the nails)

racked stretched on the rack, tortured

racking of rents raising the rent above the normal amount

realm the area ruled by the monarch, kingdom

reals Spanish silver coins

receipt refuge

recusant a Roman Catholic who refused to attend the services of the Church of England

reduce to bring to a state of

reed voice high-pitched voice

relief help and money given to a person in a state of poverty

remission a pardon, discharge of a fine

remonstrance protests, reproof

repatriate send back someone to their own country

rescripts the Queen's official edicts or announcements

retainer servant

retinue group of followers

robustious boisterous, noisy, strong

rochet smock, cloak or mantle, usually worn by bishops and abbots

rood-loft gallery above the screen, separating the choir from the nave of the church—the gallery carried a rood or cross

rood the cross as a symbol of the Christian faith

royal prerogative the exclusive power of the sovereign

ruffler vagabond

sack (verb) to loot, rob

sacrament Holy Communion

scandalise to disgrace publicly

sceptred isle island ruled by a monarch (who bears a sceptre)

schism religious rift, division, quarrel

sect of Puritans a group of Protestants known as Puritans

seditious provocative, tending to incite revolts, rebellious

Seminary a priest trained abroad

Seminaries schools or training colleges

se'night 'seven night', i.e. a week

separatist movement group of people who break away from the established order

sepulchre tomb, grave

sequester to set aside, hide

sergeants lawyers

Sheriffs royal representatives in the shires, responsible for the administration and execution of the law

shews shows, plays

shift of apparel change of clothing

shire an administrative district of the kingdom, roughly equivalent to a present-day county

shrouds sets of ropes, leading from the head of a mast, forming part of the rigging of a ship

sideways leaning 'sitting on the fence', wavering or reserving judgement

sinews strength, life-supports

solace peace and quiet, comfort

solicit to beg a favour

sore severely, seriously

sour censorers bitter critics

sovereignty supreme and independent, i.e. royal, power

special article particular and significant piece of evidence

status position, social standing

staves rods, bars, poles or large sticks

straits difficulties, hardships

strike sail lower sails as a sign of surrender

strumpet prostitute

substance possessions, goods, wealth

subversion demolition

sundry assorted, varied

suppressed put down by force

surplice a loose white garment worn by priests and choir boys taking part in church services

sustained received

swarthy dark-coloured

taciturnity silence, secrecy

take part with take sides with

Tartary the part of Eastern Europe and Asia overrun by the Tartars in the Middle Ages

testified proclaimed

testify to bear witness, swear

tillage land under cultivation

tinkers wandering beggars, traders and general performers

tippler inn keeper

tiring-house dressing-rooms in a theatre

travail effort, trouble, work

treatise literary work, composition

uncovered without a hat

under his hand a signed declaration

unseemly improper

usage custom, rules

usurp to claim illegally, or take power illegally or by force

usury lending money, charging excessive interest on a loan

utterance the disposal of goods by sale

vagrant a person who had no home and who wandered about from place to place

vassal humble and devoted servant

vasty huge

vent a market for goods

vestments priestly robes

Viceroy the person acting in the name and authority of the King or ruler

victuals food

vilest most disgusting

viols   musical instruments with five, six or seven strings, played with a bow

viva voce   by word of mouth

vocation   divine influence, or direction towards a particular career

vocation of bishops   convocation of or assembly of bishops

wanton   vulgar, suggestive, unrestrained

wardship   the guardianship of the person and lands of a minor until the child becomes of age

warp   threads placed lengthwise on a loom, across which other threads are woven

whoredom   prostitution

whoremongers   someone who has dealings with prostitutes

windermost   the furthest ship moving against the wind

wist   know

without   outside

writs   formal orders

yeoman   a countryman of respectable standing

Yeomen of the Guard   the royal body-guards

zeal   eager desire, active enthusiasm

Bibliography

'Act of the Common Council, 6 December 1574'. *Malone Society Collections,* 1908

Adams, J. C., *The Globe Playhouse,* Harvard University Press, 1943

Anderson, J. (ed.), *Collections Relating to the History of Mary, Queen of Scotland,* Vol. I, Edinburgh, 1727-8

Arber, E., *An English Garner,* Vol. IV, London, 1895

Atkinson, E. G. (ed.), *Calendar of State Papers, Ireland,* 1599-1600, HMSO

Bacon, Nathaniel, *The Annalls of Ipswiche,* W. H. Richardson (ed.), Ipswich, 1884

Bain, Joseph (ed.), *Calendar of Scottish Papers,* Vol. II, H. M. General Register House, 1900

Baldwin Smith, L., *The Elizabethan Epic,* Panther, 1969

Bindoff, S.T., *Tudor England,* Pelican, 1952

Black, J. B., *The Reign of Elizabeth,* O.U.P., 1936

Bradner, L. (ed.), *The Poems of Queen Elizabeth I,* Brown University Press, 1964

Brathwait, Richard, *The English Gentleman,* London, 1641

Breton, Nicholas, *The Works in Verse and Prose of Nicholas Breton,* Edinburgh, 1879 edition

Brown, Rawdon (ed.), *Calendar of State Papers, Venetian,* Vol. V, London, 1864-1898

Bruce, John (ed.), *Correspondence of Robert Dudley, Earl of Leicester, During His Government of the Low Counties, 1585-1586,* Camden Society, Series I, Vol. 27, 1844

Bruce, J. (ed.), *Letters of Queen Elizabeth and King James VI of Scotland,* Camden Society, 1909

Camden, William, *A History of the Most Renowned and Victorious Princess Elizabeth, Late Queen of England,* 1615, London, 1688 edition

Camden, William, *The History of the Most Renowned and Victorious Elizabeth, Late Queen of England: Selected Chapters,* W. T. MacCaffrey (ed.), University of Chicago Press, 1972

Collinson, P. (ed.), *Letters of Thomas Wood, Puritan, 1566-1577,* Bulletin of the Institute of Historical Research, Special Supplement No. 5, November 1960

Cook, D. & Wilson F.P., (eds.), *Dramatic Records in the Accounts of the Treasurer,* 1961-62

Corbett, J. S., *Drake and the Tudor Navy,* Longmans, Green & Co., 1899

Coryat, Thomas, *Crudities,* London, 1611

Cowan, I. B., *The Enigma of Mary Stuart,* Sphere Books, 1972

Dasent, John Roche (ed.), *Acts of the Privy Council,* New Series, HMSO, 1896

Devereux, W. B. (ed.), *Lives and Letters of the Devereux, Earls of Essex, in the Reigns of Elizabeth, James I and Charles I,* London, 1853

D'Ewes, Sir Simonds, *A Compleat Journal of the Votes, Speeches, Debates, both of the House of Lords and House of Commons throughout the whole reign of Queen Elizabeth of Glorious Memory,* London, 1693

Drake, Sir Francis, *The World Encompassed,* Hakluyt Society, 1854

Elton, G. R., *England Under the Tudors,* Methuen, 1965

Flecknoe, Richard, 'A Short Discourse of the English Stage', 1664, in A. M. Nagler, *A Source Book in Theatrical History,* Dover Publications, 1959

Fraser, Antonia, *Mary Queen of Scots,* Panther, 1970

Gee, Henry, *The Elizabethan Prayer Book,* London, 1902

Green, M. A. E. (ed.), *Calendar of State Papers, Domestic,* 1595-1597, London, 1869

Greg, W. W. (ed.), *Henslow's Diary,* A. H. Bullen, 1907

Hakluyt, Richard, *The Principal Navigations Voyages Traffiques and Discoveries of the English Nation,* 1589, Glasgow, 1903-4 edition

Haller, W., *The Rise of Puritanism,* Columbia University Press/O.U.P., 1938

Harington, Sir John, *Nugae Antiquae,* London, 1804

Harrison, William, *The Description of England,* 1586, George Edelen (ed.), Cornell University Press, 1968

Harrison, William, *Description of England in Shakespeare's Youth,* F. J. Furnivall (ed.), New Shakespeare Society, 1877 edition

Hentzner, Paul, *Travels in England in the Reign of Queen Elizabeth,* Cassell, 1889

Hill, Christopher, *Society and Puritanism in Pre-Revolutionary England,* Mercury Books, 1966

Hodges, Cyril Walter, *The Globe Restored: a study of the Elizabethan Theatre,* Ernest Benn, 1953

Hodges, H. W. & Hughes, E. A. (eds.), *Select Naval Documents,* Cambridge University Press, 1936

Hudson, W. & Tingey, J. C. (eds.), *Records of the City of Norwich,* Norwich, 1910

Hughes, Paul L. & Larkin, James F. (eds.), *Tudor Royal Proclamations,* Vol. I. Yale University Press, 1964

Hume, M. A. S. (ed.), *Calendar of State Papers, Spanish,* HMSO, 1892-99

Hurstfield, J., *The Queen's Wards, Wardships and Marriages under Elizabeth I,* Longmans, 1958

Jeaffreson, J. C. (ed.), *Middlesex County Records,* Vol. I, Middlesex County Records Society, 1886

Johnson, Paul, *Elizabeth: A Study in Power and Intellect,* Weidenfeld & Nicolson, 1974

Jonson, Ben, *Every Man in His Humour,* Folio edition, London, 1616

Labanoff, A. & Turnbull, A. (eds.), *Letters of Mary Stuart,* London, 1845

Lambarde, William, *Eirenarcha,* 1581, London, 1599 edition

Lee, Sidney L. (ed.), *The Autobiography of Edward, Lord Herbert of Cherbury, London,* 1886

Leslie, John, Bishop of Ross, 'A Defence of the Honour of the Right High Mighty and Noble Princess Mary, Queen of Scotland', 1569, in J. Anderson (ed.), *Collections Relating to the History of Mary, Queen of Scotland,* Vol. I, Edinburgh, 1727–8

Letters from Sir Robert Cecil to Sir George Carew, Camden Society, 1864

'Letters from the Bishops to the Privy Council', in *Camden Miscellany,* Vol. 9, Camden Society, 1895

Maisse, Andrew Herault, *Journal 1597,* G. B. Harrison and R. A. Jones (trans.), London, 1931

Markham, C. R. (ed.), *The Hawkins' Voyages During the Reigns of Henry VIII, Queen Elizabeth and James I,* Hakluyt Society, 1878

Melville, Sir James, *Memoirs of His Own Life,* Chapman & Dodd, 1922

Moorhouse, E. Hallam (ed.), *Letters of the English Seamen 1587-1808,* Chapman & Hall, 1910

Munday, A., 'A second and third blast of retreat from plays and theatres', 1580, in J. C. Adams, *The Globe Playhouse,* Harvard University Press, 1943

Nagler, A. M., *A Source Book in Theatrical History,* Dover Publications, 1959

Nashe, Thomas, *Pierce Pennilesse,* 1592, London, 1924 edition

Naunton, Sir Robert, *Fragmenta Regalia,* London, 1641

Neale, J. E., 'The Lord Keeper's speech to the parliament of 1592-3', *English Historical Review,* xxxi, 1916

Neale, J. E., *Queen Elizabeth I,* Pelican, 1971

Nuttall, Z. (ed.), *New Light on Drake: A Collection of Documents Relating to His Voyage of Circumnavigation 1577-1580* Hakluyt Society Series II, Vol. 34, 1914

Peck, F., *Desiderata Curiosa, or a collection of divers scarce and curious pieces relating chiefly to matters of English history,* London, 1779

Pound, J. F. (ed.), *The Norwich Census of the Poor,* 1570, Norfolk Record Society, 1971

Platter, Thomas, *Travels in England,* 1599, Claire Williams (trans.), Jonathan Cape, 1937 edition

Read, Conyers (ed.), *The Bardon Papers, Documents Relating to the Imprisonment and Trial of Mary Queen of Scots,* Camden Society, Third Series, Vol. 17, 1909

Read, Conyers (ed.), *William Lambarde and Local Government,* Cornell University Press, 1962

Russell, Conrad, *The Crisis of Parliaments: English History, 1509-1660,* O.U.P., 1971

Saunders, H. W. (ed.), *The Official Papers of Sir Nathaniel Bacon of Stiffkey, Norfolk, as Justice of the Peace 1580-1620,* Camden Society, Third Series, Vol. 26, 1915

Shakespeare, William, *Antony and Cleopatra*
Shakespeare, William, *Hamlet*
Shakespeare, William, *Henry V*
Shakespeare, William, *Macbeth*

Shakespeare, William, *Merchant of Venice*
Shakespeare, William, *Richard II*

Smith, Sir Thomas, *De Republica Anglorum, A Discourse on the Commonwealth of England,* L. Alston (ed.), Cambridge University Press, 1907

Statutes of the Realm, Vol. IV, London 1819

Stephens, H. Morse, *Portugal,* T. Fisher Unwin, 1891

Stone, L., *The Crisis of the Aristocracy 1558-1641* O.U.P., 1965

Stow, John, *A Survey of London,* 1603, Charles L. Kingsford (ed.), Clarendon Press, 1908

Strachey, Lytton, *Elizabeth and Essex,* Chatto & Windus, 1928

Strype, John, *Annals of the Reformation and Establishment of Religion and other Various Occurrences in the Church of England during Queen Elizabeth's Happy Reign,* London, 1725

Strype, John, *The Life of Sir Thomas Smith,* Oxford, 1820

Tawney, R. H., & Power, E. (eds.), *Tudor Economic Documents,* Vol III, Longmans, 1951

Viles, Edward & Furnivall, F. J. (eds.), *The Rogues and Vagabonds of Shakespeare's Youth,* New Shakespeare Society, 1880

von Klarwill, Victor, *Queen Elizabeth and Some Foreigners,* T. H. Nash (trans.), Bodley, 1928 edition

Waugh, Evelyn, *Edmund Campion,* Penguin, 1953

Williams, Neville, *All the Queen's Men,* Cardinal, 1974

Wilson, John Dover (ed.), *Life in Shakespeare's England,* Penguin, 1968

Acknowledgements

The authors and publishers are grateful to the following for permission to reproduce copyright material:

Photographs and illustrations

Front cover *Alfresco Music,* from Edmund Spenser's *Shepherd's Calendar,* reproduced by permission of the British Library Board; page 4 *Bull and bear baiting,* John Freeman; page 7 *The rich man and the poor man,* Mansell Collection; page 8 *Henry VIII & Anne Boleyn* National Portrait Gallery; London; page 9 *Elizabeth, the Ermine portrait & Elizabeth, the Rainbow portrait,* by courtesy of the Marquess of Salisbury; page 10 *The Queen proceeding to Westminster,* The College of Arms; page 11 *Roger Ascham,* National Portrait Gallery; page 12 *Mary Tudor,* National Portrait Gallery; page 13 *Elizabeth as a princess,* reproduced by gracious permission of Her Majesty The Queen; page 14 *Elizabeth carried by courtiers,* Mr. Simon Wingfield Digby, Sherborne Castle; page 16 *Elizabeth with advisers,* Mary Evans Picture Library; page 19 *Sir William Cecil,* courtesy of the Marquess of Salisbury; page 20 *Elizabeth with Privy Councillors,* Mary Evans Picture Library; page 22 *Earl of Leicester,* The Trustees of the Wallace Collection; page 23 *Earl of Essex,* The Trustees of the National Gallery of Ireland; page 24 *Earl of Leicester,* National Portrait Gallery; page 25 *The Spanish Ambassador,* Mansell Collection; page 26 *Sir Francis Walsingham,* National Portrait Gallery; page 27 *Elizabeth with Dutch ambassadors,* Staatliche Kunstsammlungen, Kassel; page 28 *Westminster,* Mansell Collection; page 31 *Elizabeth, the Armada portrait,* from the Woburn Abbey Collection, by kind permission of His Grace The Duke of Bedford, The Marquess of Tavistock and the Trustees of the Bedford Estates; page 32 *The Queen in Parliament,* by permission of the British Library Board; page 33 *Proclamation by the Earl of Sussex,* by permission of the British Library Board; page 35 *Sir Simonds D'Ewes Journal,* by permission of the British Library Board; page 37 *Man in the pillory,* Mansell Collection; page 39 *Court of Star Chamber & Trial in Westminster Hall,* Mansell Collection; page 40 *Corporal punishments,* Radio Times Hulton Picture Library; *Punishment in Lollard's Tower,* Mary Evans Picture Library; page 42 *Four beggars,* Historical Picture Service; page 43 *A lady spinning,* Mansell Collection; page 44 *Caveat for Common Cursetors,* by permission of the British Library Board; : page 45 *Various beggars,* Radio Times Hulton Picture Library; page 46 *Pinseller,* Mary Evans Picture Library; page 47 *Ratcatcher,* Historical Picture Service; page 48 *Stoneware for sale & A ballad singer,* Mary Evans Picture Library; page 49 *Southwark Gate,* Mansell Collection; page 50 *The brank & The Beggar being whipped,* Mary Evans Picture Library; page 52 *John Cottington,* Radio Times Hulton Picture Library; page 53 *A beggar,* Historical Picture Service; page 54 *Women going to market,* Mansell Collection; page 55 *The Almonry,* Popperfoto; page 56 *Examples of punishments,* John Freeman; page 57 *Beggars,* John Freeman; *A persistent beggar,* Mansell Collection; page 58 *People in the stocks,* Mary Evans Picture Library; page 59 *The Protestant Succession,* from the collection at Sudeley Castle, Winchcombe, Gloucestershire; page 61 *The burning of the heretics,* Mansell Collection; *Execution of Catholics,* Radio Times Hulton Picture Library; page 62 *Elizabeth going to St. Paul's,* Mary Evans Picture Library; page 63 *Matthew Parker,* by courtesy of the Archbishop of Canterbury; Copyright reserved by The Courtauld Institute of Art and The Church Commissioners; page 64 *Philip II,* National Portrait Gallery; page 65 *The Pope,* Radio Times Hulton Picture Library; page 67 *Father Parsons and Father Campion,* Mary Evans Picture Library; page 68 *William Parry,* Radio Times Hulton Picture Library; page 71 *Man being tortured,* Radio Times Hulton Picture Library; page 73 *The Spanish Armada,* Popperfoto; page 75 *A chart of the battle,* Mary Evans Picture Library; page 76 *Drake commanding the Revenge,* Radio Times Hulton Picture Library; page 79 *A Puritan family,* Mansell Collection; page 80 *John Goodwin,* Mansell Collection; page 81 *John Knox & His signature,* Mansell Collection; page 82 *The descent of the Pope,* Mansell Collection; page 84 *John Stubbs,* Mary Evans Picture Library; page 85 *John*

Whitgift, Mansell Collection; page 87 *The Arms of Mary* by permission of the British Library Board; *A letter by Mary,* The Keeper of the Records of Scotland; page 88 *Mary wearing a bonnet,* National Portrait Gallery; *Mary & Francis II,* Bibliotheque Nationale; page 89 *Elizabeth standing on a map,* National Portrait Gallery; page 90 *Thomas Howard,* National Portrait Gallery; page 91 *Darnley's murder,* Public Record Office, London; *Mary and Darnley,* Mansell Collection; page 92 *Tutbury Castle,* by permission of the British Library Board; page 93 *Mary, the Deuil Blanc portrait,* The Trustees of the Scottish National Portrait Gallery; *Mary during her imprisonment,* D. E. Bower Collection, Chiddingstone Castle; page 94 *Ridolfi Plot,* Radio Times Hulton Picture Library; page 95 *St. Bartholomews Day Massacre,* Mansell Collection; page 96 *Mary, a miniature,* Victoria and Albert Museum, Crown copyright; *Mary, a medal,* by courtesy of the Trustees of the British Museum; page 97 *The Throckmorton Plot,* Radio Times Hulton Picture Library; *Assassination of William,* Mansell Collection; page 98 *Sir Christopher Hatton,* National Portrait Gallery; page 99 *Elizabeth I,* National Portrait Gallery; page 100 *The trial of Mary,* Courtesy of the trustees of the British Museum; page 101 *Mary's embroidery,* Victoria and Albert Museum, Crown copyright; page 102 *Mary in captivity,* Radio Times Hulton Picture Library; page 103 *Mary, a memorial portrait,* Blairs College, Aberdeen; *The Earl of Shrewsbury,* The National Trust & The Courtauld Institute of Art; page 104 *Bess of Hardwick,* National Portrait Gallery; *The execution,* The Trustees of the British Museum; page 106 *The execution,* Blairs College, Aberdeen; page 107 *The effigy,* by courtesy of the Dean and Chapter of Westminster; page 108 *George Gascoigne,* Mansell Collection page 109 *A conjuror,* Mary Evans Picture Library; page 111 *Edward Alleyn,* Mary Evans Picture Library; page 112 *Palladio's plan,* by permission of the British Library Board; page 113 *An Elizabethan stage,* from C. Walter Hodges, *The Globe Restored,* O.U.P.; *The Fortune theatre,* Mansell Collection; page 114 *Shakespeare,* Mansell Collection; page 115 *The Swan theatre,* The Library of the Riksuniversiteit, Utrecht; page 116 *A circus performance,* Mansell Collection; page 117 *The stage at the Globe,* R. W. Yates; page 118 *A mime,* Mansell Collection; page 119 *Crowds arriving at the Globe,* Mansell Collection; page 120 *A performance at the Globe,* Radio Times Hulton Picture Library; page 122 *Will Kempe,* Mansell Collection; page 123 *Richard Burbage,* Mary Evans Picture Library; page 125 *Aristocrats in the audience,* Radio Times Hulton Picture Library; page 126 *Ben Jonson,* Mansell Collection; page 127 *Spanish shipbuilding plans,* Museo Naval, Madrid; page 128 *Map of the World,* Radio Times Hulton Picture Library; page 129 *Sir Humphrey Gilbert,* Mansell Collection; page 130 *The route to the Far East,* Mansell Collection; page 133 *Sir John Hawkins,* Mansell Collection; page 134 *Sir Francis Drake,* Radio Times Hulton Picture Library; page 136 *The Golden Hind,* Radio Times Hulton Picture Library; page 137 *An Elizabethan pinnace,* Radio Times Hulton Picture Library; page 139 *A Mariner's mirror,* by permission of the British Library Board; page 141 *Drawing of a mariner's mirror,* by permission of the British Library Board; page 142 *A Spanish shipbuilding plan,* Museo Naval, Madrid; page 143 *The Great Harry,* Mansell Collection; page 144 *Map showing Drake's circumnavigation,* Mansell Collection; page 145 *Lord Howard of Effingham,* Mary Evans Picture Library; page 146 *The Ark Royal,* courtesy of the Trustees of the British Museum; page 147 *An Elizabethan galleon,* National Maritime Museum, London; page 148 *An Elizabethan ship,* Radio Times Hulton Picture Library; *Hanseatic League depot,* Mary Evans Picture Library; page 152 *Raleigh attacks a port,* Radio Times Hulton Picture Library; page 153 *Raleigh lands in Virginia,* Radio Times Hulton Picture Library; *An Indian Chief,* courtesy of the Trustees of the British Museum; page 154 *A lady dancing with Leicester,* by permission of Viscount De L'Isle, VC, KG, from his collection at Penshurst Place, Kent; page 155 *The Earl of Essex,* National Portrait Gallery; page 156 *The Earl of Essex,* from the Woburn Abbey Collection, by kind permission of His Grace The Duke of Bedford, the Marquess of Tavistock, and the Trustees of the Bedford Estates; page 157 *The death warrant,* by courtesy of His Grace The Duke of Sutherland, and the Trustees of the British Museum; page 158 *A map showing Essex House,* Mansell Collection; page 159 *Essex*

House from the Thames, Mansell Collection; page 160 *Elizabeth at Wanstead,* The Duke of Portland, Welbeck Abbey, page 161 *The Earl of Essex,* National Portrait Gallery; page 162 *Burghley and Cecil,* by courtesy of the Marquess of Salisbury; page 165 *Time and Death,* The Lord Methuen; page 167 *The Earl of Southampton,* The Duke of Buccleuch and Queensbury; page 168 *The Gunpowder Plot,* National Portrait Gallery; Back cover *The south bank of the Thames,* Mansell Collection.

Extracts

Source 3 Sir James Melville, *Memoirs of His Own Life,* Chapman & Dodd; Sources 5, 92 Paul Johnson, *Elizabeth: A Study in Power and Intellect,* Weidenfeld & Nicolson; Sources 12, 245 Neville Williams, *All the Queen's Men,* Weidenfeld & Nicolson; Sources 30, 31, 32, 37, 43, 44, 45, 46, 48, 49 L. Alston (ed.), *De Republica Anglorum, A Discourse on the Commonwealth of England,* Cambridge University Press; Source 35 The Editor, *English Historical Review* and The Longman Group Limited; Source 39 Paul L. Hughes & James F. Larkin (eds.), *Tudor Royal Proclamations,* Yale University Press; Sources 41, 58 Conyers Read (ed.), *William Lambarde and Local Government,* The Folger Library and the University Press of Virginia; Source 42 William Harrison, *The Description of England,* The University Press of Virginia; Sources 47, 50, 55, 61, 167, 241, 242 William Harrison, *The Description of England,* The University Press of Virginia; Source 51 Christopher Hill, *Society and Puritanism in Pre-Revolutionary England,* Martin Secker & Warburg Limited; Source 57 Conrad Russell, *The Crisis of Parliaments: English History 1509-1660,* by permission of the Oxford University Press; Source 66 Norfolk Record Society; Sources 97, 99, 100, 101, 106 Evelyn Waugh, *Edmund Campion,* Reprinted by permission of A.D Peters & Co Ltd; Sources 104, 105, 108,114, 115, 116, 122, 124, 129, 130 William Camden, *The History of the most Renowned and Victorious Princess Elizabeth,* W. T. MacCaffrey (ed.), University of Chicago Press, 1970 ©1970 by The University of Chicago; Source 125 Professor Patrick Collinson and the Editor, *Bulletin of the Institute of Historical Research;* Source 126 W. Haller, *The Rise of Puritanism,* by permission of the Oxford University Press; Sources 136, 140, 148, 154 Antonia Fraser, *Mary Queen of Scots,* Weidenfeld & Nicolson; Source 141 I. B. Cowan; Sources 142, 165 S. T. Bindoff, *Tudor England* (Pelican History of England, 1950) pp. 207, 245-246 copyright © S. T. Bindoff, 1950 Reprinted by permission of Penguin Books Ltd; Source 143 Reprinted from *The Poems of Queen Elizabeth I,* edited by Leicester Bradner, Brown University Press, 1964. © Brown University; Source 147 Lacey Baldwin Smith, *The Elizabethan Epic,* Jonathan Cape Ltd; Source 153 the Executors of the J. E. Neale Estate, *Queen Elizabeth I,* Jonathan Cape Ltd; Source 166 G. R. Elton, *England Under the Tudors,* Methuen & Co; Source 171 Cyril Walter Hodges, *The Globe Restored: a Study of the Elizabethan Theatre,* Ernest Benn Limited; Source 176 Victor von Klarwill, *Queen Elizabeth and Some Foreigners,* T. H. Nash (trans.), The Bodley Head; Source 184 John Dover Wilson (ed.), *Life in Shakespeare's England,* Cambridge University Press; Source 188 Clare Williams, *Thomas Platter's Travels in England,* Jonathan Cape Ltd; Source 190 J. C. Adams, *The Globe Playhouse,* Harvard University Press, 1943; Source 195 A. M. Nagler, *A Source Book in Theatrical History* 1959, Dover Publications Inc; Sources 232, 233, 235, 237, 238 H. W. Hodges & E. A. Hughes (eds.), *Select Naval Documents,* Cambridge University Press; Source 240 E. Hallam Moorhouse (ed.), *Letters of the English Seamen 1587-1808,* Chapman & Hall; Sources 246, 247 Lytton Strachey, *Elizabeth and Essex,* the author's literary estate, Chatto and Windus Ltd; Sources 252, 260 L. Stone, *The Crisis of the Aristocracy 1558-1641,* by permission of the Oxford University Press; Source 263 J. B. Black, *The Reign of Elizabeth 1558-1603,* by permission of the Oxford University Press.

BACK COVER: The south bank of the Thames, an engraving by Hollar c. 1647